Meredith® Press
Des Moines, Iowa

**Meredith Press**
**An imprint of Meredith® Books**

**Heartland Baking**
Editor: Kristi Fuller
Contributing Editors: Spectrum Communication Services, Inc.
Associate Art Director: Lynda Haupert
Copy Chief: Angela K. Renkoski
Test Kitchen Director: Sharon Stilwell
Photographers: Ron Crofoot, Mike Dieter, Scott Little
Electronic Production Coordinator: Paula Forest
Editorial and Design Assistants: Judy Bailey, Jennifer Norris, Karen Schirm
Production Director: Douglas M. Johnston
Production Manager: Pam Kvitne
Prepress Coordinator: Marjorie J. Schenkelberg

**Meredith® Books**
Editor in Chief: James D. Blume
Design Director: Matt Strelecki
Managing Editor: Gregory H. Kayko
Executive Food Editor: Lisa Holderness

Vice President, General Manager: Jamie L. Martin

**Meredith Publishing Group**
President, Publishing Group: Christopher M. Little
Vice President and Publishing Director: John P. Loughlin

**Meredith Corporation**
Chairman of the Board: Jack D. Rehm
President and Chief Executive Officer: William T. Kerr

Chairman of the Executive Committee: E.T. Meredith III

Cover Design: Daniel Pelavin
Cover photograph: Never-Fail Cinnamon Rolls, recipe on *page 88*
Photographer: Mike Dieter
Natural Selection Stock Photography, Inc., © K. Collins, *pages 4-5*
Natural Selection Stock Photography, Inc., © Gil Lopez-Espina, *page 56*
© Stock Imagery/Airphoto, *page 46*
© Stock Imagery/Westmorland, *page 6*

All of us at Meredith® Books are dedicated to providing you with the information and
ideas you need to create delicious foods. We welcome your comments and suggestions.
Write to us at: Meredith® Books, Cookbook Editorial Department, RW-240, 1716 Locust
St., Des Moines, IA 50309-3023.

Our seal assures you that every recipe in *Heartland Baking* has been
tested in the Better Homes and Gardens® Test Kitchen. This
means that each recipe is practical and reliable, and meets our high
standards of taste appeal. We guarantee your satisfaction with this
book for as long as you own it.

**B**aking treats for family and friends is a satisfying labor of love for many cooks. And nobody knows baking like cooks from the Heartland, where ingredients are farm fresh and sharing food is the focus of many gatherings. Here, in this special cookbook, you'll find the best recipes from Midwestern homes, restaurants, and inns—from Michigan to Missouri, Ohio to Kansas—all selected by the editors of *Midwest Living*® magazine.

In this keepsake cookbook, you'll discover a cache of old-fashioned favorites and baking tips that will help make your efforts a success every time. All recipes have been tested and approved by the Better Homes and Gardens® Test Kitchen, which means you'll be assured of getting the best results.

Our three chapters—Everyday Treasures, Prizewinning Pleasures, and Special-Day Delights—have just the right cookie, cake, pie, or bread for your particular occasion or craving. Each chapter opens with a mini index, so locating a specific type of recipe is easy. Your biggest challenge will be choosing which mouthwatering recipe to make next! So, roll up your sleeves, don your apron, and start baking some fragrant goodies to share and enjoy with your own family and friends.

# CONTENTS ▲▲▲▲▲▲▲▲▲

# EVERYDAY TREASURES

**S**ome days you're in the mood to bake something yummy—just because. In this chapter, you'll find an assortment of baked goodies that fit the bill.

*Numbers in italic type indicate a photograph.*

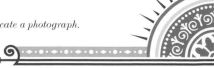

# SOUR CREAM-NUTMEG SOFTIES

 rdith Fischer's family in Owen, Wisconsin, loves soft sugar cookies. Though Ardith never found the recipe for her grandmother's cookies, which she remembers fondly, this one comes close.

- 4 cups all-purpose flour
- 1 teaspoon baking soda
- 1 teaspoon ground nutmeg
- ½ teaspoon salt
- ½ cup butter
- ½ cup shortening or lard
- 1½ cups sugar
- 1 egg
- 1 8-ounce carton dairy sour cream
- 1 teaspoon vanilla
- Powdered Sugar Icing (recipe follows; optional)
- Crushed peppermint candies, decorative candies and/or colored sugar (optional)

1 Stir together flour, baking soda, nutmeg and salt. Set aside. In a large mixing bowl, beat butter and shortening till softened. Add sugar and beat till fluffy. Add egg, sour cream and vanilla. Beat mixture well.

2 Add the flour mixture to butter mixture; beat or stir well. (Dough will be sticky.) Cover dough and refrigerate several hours or till dough is easy to handle.

3 On a lightly floured surface, roll *one-third* of the dough at a time to ¼-inch thickness. Cut into desired shapes with 2- to 3-inch cookie cutters. Place on ungreased cookie sheets.

4 Bake in a 350° oven about 10 minutes or till edges of cookies are firm and bottoms are golden. Transfer cookies to wire racks; cool.

5 If you like, frost with Powdered Sugar Icing and decorate with peppermint candies, decorative candies and/or colored sugar. Makes 60 to 72 cookies.

**Powdered Sugar Icing:** In a medium mixing bowl, mix 2 cups sifted *powdered sugar* and ½ teaspoon *vanilla*. Stir in enough *milk, 1 tablespoon* at a time, to make a spreadable consistency. If you like, tint some of the icing with *pastel food coloring* and use to pipe on decorative accents.

# CHOCOLATE-OATMEAL COOKIES

 ilk chocolate and semisweet chocolate fill these hefty cookies from the Knollwood House bed-and-breakfast in River Falls, Wisconsin. A mint-chocolate or candy coating drizzle adds a festive finish.

- 1¼ cups packed brown sugar
- 1 cup sugar
- ½ cup butter
- 3 eggs
- ¾ cup peanut butter
- 1 teaspoon vanilla
- 2 teaspoons baking soda
- 4½ cups quick-cooking rolled oats
- ½ cup chopped walnuts
- ½ cup candy-coated milk chocolate pieces
- ¼ cup semisweet chocolate pieces
- Mint-Chocolate Drizzle (recipe follows)
- Candy Coating Drizzle (recipe follows)

1 In a large bowl, beat brown sugar, sugar and butter with electric mixer till thoroughly combined.

2 Add eggs; beat well. Beat in peanut butter and vanilla till thoroughly combined. Beat in baking soda. By hand, stir in rolled oats, walnuts, milk chocolate pieces and semisweet chocolate pieces.

3 Using ¼ cup of dough for each cookie, drop dough 3 inches apart onto ungreased cookie sheets. Flatten each slightly. Bake in a 350° oven for 13 to 15 minutes or till edges are firm. Let cool on cookie sheets for 1 minute. Transfer to wire racks; cool completely.

4 Decorate with Mint-Chocolate Drizzle or Candy Coating Drizzle or both. Makes 24 cookies.

**Mint-Chocolate Drizzle:** In a small saucepan, melt together ½ cup *mint-flavored semisweet chocolate pieces* and 1 teaspoon *shortening*.

**Candy Coating Drizzle:** Melt 4 ounces *vanilla-flavored candy coating*.

# ALMOND CRUNCH COOKIES

**C**hef Moose Zader from Silver Dollar City near Branson, Missouri, stirs almond brickle into these slice-and-bake cookies. This makes a big batch. If you like, keep a portion of the dough in the freezer for fresh, hot cookies anytime.*

1½ cups shortening
1 cup sugar
1 cup packed brown sugar
3 eggs
1½ teaspoons baking soda
1 teaspoon vanilla

¼ teaspoon salt
3½ cups all-purpose flour
1 7½-ounce package
(1⅓ cups) almond brickle pieces

**1** In a large mixing bowl, beat shortening, sugar and brown sugar with an electric mixer till thoroughly combined. Add eggs; beat well. Add baking soda, vanilla and salt; beat well. Add the flour. Beat or stir till combined. Stir in almond brickle pieces.

**2** Divide dough into four portions. On a lightly floured surface, with lightly floured hands, roll each portion into a 12×1½-inch log (dough will be soft). Wrap and place logs of cookie dough on a cookie sheet; refrigerate for 4 to 24 hours or freeze for 1 hour.

**3** Remove one log of dough from the refrigerator. Cut into ½-inch-thick slices; place on ungreased cookie sheets. Flatten cookies slightly with the bottom of a glass dipped in sugar.

**4** Bake in a 350° oven for 8 to 10 minutes or till the edges are lightly browned. Cool 1 minute. Transfer to wire racks; cool. Makes about 80 cookies.

***Note**: To freeze dough, individually wrap log(s) in plastic wrap; place in an airtight container. Freeze dough for up to 6 months. To use, thaw dough just until soft enough to slice.

# GRANDPA'S SNICKER-DOODLES

**W**hen she was a child, Lisa Blouin of Belleville, Illinois, spent summers with her grandparents in Des Moines. Lisa fondly remembers evening desserts, including these cookies Grandpa made.

1½ cups all-purpose flour
1 teaspoon ground cinnamon
½ teaspoon baking soda
½ cup shortening, melted
⅓ cup sugar

⅓ cup packed brown sugar
1 beaten egg
½ teaspoon vanilla
2 tablespoons sugar
¼ teaspoon ground cinnamon

**1** In a medium mixing bowl, stir together the flour, 1 teaspoon cinnamon and baking soda. Set aside.

**2** In a large mixing bowl, stir together the shortening, ⅓ cup sugar and brown sugar till combined. Stir in egg and vanilla till combined. Stir in the flour mixture.

**3** Lightly grease cookie sheets. Set aside. Stir together the 2 tablespoons sugar and ¼ teaspoon cinnamon. Shape dough into 36 one-inch balls; roll each ball in the sugar-cinnamon mixture. Place on the prepared cookie sheets about 2 inches apart. Flatten each ball by crisscrossing with tines of a fork.

**4** Bake in a 375° oven for 6 to 8 minutes or till edges are golden brown. Transfer cookies to wire racks; cool. Makes 36 cookies.

# HUNKA CHOCOLATE COOKIES

The ultimate chocolate cookie. If one of these giant fudgies is too much for you, share it with someone. You may also make the cookies smaller if you like, but reduce the baking time by a few minutes. (Pictured on page 11.)

2 12-ounce packages
    (4 cups) semisweet
    chocolate pieces
4 ounces unsweetened
    chocolate
¼ cup butter
½ cup all-purpose flour
½ teaspoon baking powder
¼ teaspoon salt

4 eggs
1⅓ cups sugar
2 teaspoons vanilla
2 to 3 cups broken walnuts,
    toasted
    White baking bar, melted
    Semisweet chocolate,
    melted

**1** In a heavy saucepan, heat *1 package* of the semisweet chocolate pieces, the unsweetened chocolate and butter over low heat till melted, stirring constantly. Transfer to a large bowl; cool slightly.

**2** In a bowl, stir together the flour, baking powder and salt. Set aside.

**3** Add eggs, sugar and vanilla to chocolate mixture. Beat with an electric mixer till combined. Add flour mixture and beat on low speed till well combined. Stir in remaining chocolate pieces and walnuts.

**4** Lightly grease cookie sheets. Using ¼ *cup* of dough for each cookie, drop 3 inches apart onto prepared cookie sheets. Flatten each cookie slightly.

**5** Bake in a 350° oven for 12 to 15 minutes or till edges are firm and surface is dull and cracked. Cool 2 minutes. Transfer cookies to wire racks; cool.

**6** Drizzle cookies with melted white baking bar and melted semisweet chocolate. Makes 24 cookies.

---

# TANGY OLD-FASHIONED LEMON BARS

In quaint Long Grove, Illinois, you can visit the Farmside Country Store, where jars of homemade lemon curd and other food gifts fill the shelves. The store's bakery uses Lemon Curd for these delicious bars. (Pictured on page 11.)

Lemon Curd (recipe
    follows) or 1½ cups
    purchased lemon curd
2 cups all-purpose flour
1 cup sugar

½ teaspoon baking soda
1 cup unsalted butter
    or regular butter
⅔ cup coconut
½ cup chopped nuts, such
    as pecans, toasted

**1** Prepare Lemon Curd. Set aside. In a large bowl, combine flour, sugar and baking soda. Using a pastry blender, cut in butter till crumbly. Set aside *1½ cups* of the flour mixture.

**2** For crust, press the remaining flour mixture into the bottom of an ungreased 13×9×2-inch baking pan. Bake in a 375° oven for 10 minutes. Cool crust in pan on wire rack for 10 minutes.

**3** Reduce the oven temperature to 350°. Spread Lemon Curd over the partially cooled crust. Combine reserved crumb mixture with the coconut and nuts. Sprinkle over lemon layer.

**4** Bake in the 350° oven for 20 to 25 minutes or till golden brown. Cool in pan on wire rack. Cut into triangles or bars. Makes 40 bars.

**Lemon Curd:** In a heavy small saucepan, combine ⅔ cup *sugar* and ½ cup *butter*. Heat and stir till combined. Slowly whisk in 3 beaten *egg yolks* and ¼ cup *lemon juice*. Cook and stir over low to medium heat for 5 to 7 minutes or till thick and just bubbling. Transfer to bowl. Cover surface with plastic wrap. Cool for 30 minutes. Makes 1½ cups.

TANGY OLD-FASHIONED LEMON
BARS (back plate, see recipe, page 10) AND
RASPBERRY CHEESECAKE BARS
(back plate, see recipe, page 17)
SPICY PUMPKIN COOKIES (front plate,
see recipe, page 16) AND HUNKA
CHOCOLATE COOKIES (front plate, see
recipe, page 10)

# MAPLE-OATMEAL COOKIES

These nutty raisin-studded treats will disappear fast from your cookie jar. The recipe for the soft, cakey cookies comes from the collection of the Reynolds family in Aniwa, Wisconsin. The maple flavor really shines through.

1 cup pure maple syrup
½ cup shortening
1 egg
1½ cups all-purpose flour
2 teaspoons baking powder
½ teaspoon salt
¼ cup milk
1½ cups rolled oats
½ cup raisins
½ cup chopped walnuts or pecans

**1** In a large mixing bowl, beat the maple syrup, shortening and egg with an electric mixer till thoroughly combined.

**2** In another mixing bowl, stir together the flour, baking powder and salt. Add the flour mixture and milk alternately to the syrup mixture, beating after each addition till just combined. Stir in the rolled oats, raisins and chopped walnuts or pecans.

**3** Lightly grease cookie sheets. Drop dough by tablespoonfuls onto prepared cookie sheets. Bake cookies in a 350° oven for 10 to 12 minutes or till the edges are lightly browned. Transfer to wire racks; cool. Makes about 40 cookies.

# KAREN'S CHEESECAKE BARS

For a decorative touch, Karen Flemal of Sun Prairie, Wisconsin, sometimes cuts these miniature cheesecakes into triangular shapes instead of bars. Sprinkle fresh raspberries over each serving for a colorful dessert.

5 tablespoons butter
⅓ cup packed brown sugar
1 cup all-purpose flour
¼ cup chopped walnuts
1 8-ounce package cream cheese
½ cup sugar
1 egg
2 tablespoons milk
1 to 2 tablespoons lemon juice
½ teaspoon vanilla

**1** In a mixing bowl, beat butter with an electric mixer for 30 seconds or till softened. Add the brown sugar and beat till fluffy. Beat in flour and walnuts. Set aside *1 cup* of the butter mixture.

**2** Press the remaining butter mixture into bottom of an ungreased 8×8×2-inch baking pan. Bake in a 350° oven for 12 minutes.

**3** Meanwhile, beat together the cream cheese and sugar. Add the egg, milk, lemon juice and vanilla; mix well. Pour over baked layer in pan.

**4** Sprinkle the reserved butter mixture over top. Bake in 350° oven for 25 minutes. Cool in pan on wire rack. Cut into bars. Cover and store in the refrigerator. Makes 28 bars.

# CHOCOLATE-NUT REVELS

ary Ellen Beaver of Connersville, Indiana, has been shaping and baking these chocolate-swirl cookies for family and friends since the 1960s. Just a few simple on-hand ingredients create this mouthwatering treat.

1 6-ounce package (1 cup) semisweet chocolate pieces
1 cup chopped pecans
1 cup butter

⅔ cup sugar
1 teaspoon vanilla
¼ teaspoon salt
2 cups all-purpose flour
  Sugar

1 In a heavy saucepan, melt chocolate over low heat. Stir in pecans.

2 In a large mixing bowl, beat butter with an electric mixer about 30 seconds or till softened. Add the ⅔ cup sugar and beat till fluffy. Beat in vanilla and salt. Add flour; beat or stir till mixed.

3 Spoon chocolate mixture over dough. Stir till just marbled. Drop the cookie dough by rounded teaspoonfuls 2 inches apart onto ungreased cookie sheets. If you like, roll each mound into a ball for more even edges. Grease bottom of a glass. For each cookie, dip glass in sugar and press cookie to ¼-inch thickness.

4 Bake in a 350° oven for 10 to 12 minutes or till cookies are set. Cool on cookie sheets for 1 minute. Transfer the cookies to wire racks; cool. Makes about 36 cookies.

## Tried-and-True Baking Tips

Midwestern cooks are well known for their exceptional baked goods. Part of the reason they're so successful is that they know these tricks of the baking trade:

♦ Preheat your oven before you mix the ingredients for baked goods. (For yeast breads, preheat the oven after dough rises.) Check your oven temperature occasionally with an oven thermometer to make sure it's accurate.

♦ Choose your bakeware according to its browning ability. Shiny bakeware reflects heat and slows the browning process, making it ideal for shortbread and soft crust breads. Cookware with a dull finish and glass baking dishes will absorb more heat and brown crusts much quicker, which is perfect for piecrusts, cookies, coffee cakes and crusty breads.

♦ Grease muffin cups and loaf pans on the bottoms and only halfway up the sides to prevent formation of rims around the edges of quick breads.

♦ For even baking, bake on only one rack of your oven and allow space between baking sheets, pans or dishes for the warm air to circulate.

♦ To avoid soggy sides and bottoms, cool baked goods in the pans only as long as the recipe directs, then transfer them to a wire rack to finish cooling.

# Double Chocolate-Mint Shortbread

These rich, melt-in-your-mouth shortbread cookies make a noteworthy addition to holiday cookie trays. The lacy drizzle isn't mandatory, but it adds a festive flair.

¾ cup butter
1⅓ cups all-purpose flour
¾ cup sifted powdered
    sugar
¼ cup unsweetened cocoa
    powder
¼ teaspoon mint extract
¾ cup miniature semisweet
    chocolate pieces

Chocolate-flavored candy
    coating and/or
    vanilla-flavored green
    candy coating, melted
    (optional)
Crushed mint candies
    (optional)

1 In a large mixing bowl, beat butter with an electric mixer about 30 seconds or till softened. Add about *half* of the flour, the powdered sugar, cocoa powder and mint extract. Beat well. Stir in the remaining flour. Stir in the chocolate pieces. If necessary, refrigerate dough for 1 to 2 hours or till easy to handle.

2 Lightly grease a cookie sheet. On the prepared cookie sheet, pat the dough into a 9-inch circle. Using your fingers, press to make a scalloped edge. With a fork, prick dough deeply to make 16 wedges.

3 Bake in a 300° oven about 25 minutes or till edges are firm to the touch and center is set. Let cool for 2 minutes on the cookie sheet. With a long, sharp knife, cut along the fork pricks into wedges. Carefully transfer to a wire rack to cool.

4 If you like, drizzle with melted candy coating; sprinkle with crushed candies before the coating dries. Makes 16 servings.

## Butter vs. Margarine

Because so many areas of the Midwest are dotted with dairy farms, high-quality butter, cheese and other dairy products have long been a tradition in the Heartland. The best bakers know that using butter gives baked goods a rich flavor and pleasing texture. To match their top-notch results, take a tip from them and use butter in your cookies, cakes, pastries and breads. If you choose to use margarine or a stick spread instead, be sure to select a product that is at least 60 percent vegetable oil. Do not use an "extra light" spread that contains only about 40 percent oil.

# SPICY PUMPKIN COOKIES

umpkin is a Midwestern favorite, especially when it's used in irresistible treats such as these cakelike cookies, which are topped with a brown sugar glaze. Canned pumpkin makes the cookies a snap to stir together. (Pictured on page 11.)

1 cup shortening
1 cup sugar
1 cup canned pumpkin
1 egg
2 cups all-purpose flour
1 tablespoon pumpkin pie
   spice
½ teaspoon baking powder
¼ teaspoon baking soda
   Cookie Glaze (recipe
   follows)
   Chopped nuts (optional)

1 In an extra-large mixing bowl, beat together shortening and sugar with an electric mixer till fluffy. Add pumpkin and egg; beat till combined.

2 In another bowl, combine flour, pumpkin pie spice, baking powder and baking soda. Beat into the pumpkin mixture till combined.

3 Spoon by rounded teaspoonfuls onto ungreased cookie sheets.

4 Bake cookies in a 375° oven for 8 to 10 minutes or till the tops seem firm. Transfer to wire racks; cool.

5 Prepare Cookie Glaze. Spread over the cookies. If you like, sprinkle with nuts. Makes 42 to 48 cookies.

**Cookie Glaze:** In a medium saucepan, combine ½ cup packed *brown sugar*, 3 tablespoons *butter* and 1 tablespoon *milk*. Heat over medium heat till butter melts, stirring occasionally. Remove from heat. Stir in 1 cup sifted *powdered sugar* and 1 teaspoon *vanilla*. (If frosting is too thick, stir in a few drops of *hot water*.)

# CHOCOLATE-TOFFEE CANDY COOKIES

anet Barnhill, who lives at Missouri's Whiteman Air Force Base, says these layered cookies taste like miniature toffee bars. For snack time emergencies, keep these simple five ingredients on hand for the next batch.

  About 35 saltine crackers
1 cup butter
1 cup packed brown sugar
1 11½-ounce package milk
   chocolate pieces
1 cup chopped nuts

1 Line a 15×10×1-inch baking pan with foil. Place crackers in a single layer to cover bottom of pan. (If necessary, break crackers to fit.)

2 In a medium saucepan, combine butter and brown sugar. Heat and stir over medium heat till mixture boils; boil gently for 3 minutes. Pour butter mixture evenly over crackers. Bake in 375° oven for 5 minutes.

3 Remove from oven; sprinkle with milk chocolate pieces. Let stand for a few minutes till melted; spread chocolate evenly over all.

4 Sprinkle with nuts, pressing them in lightly. Cool in pan on wire rack. Cover and refrigerate. To serve, cut into squares or diamonds. Makes 48 cookies.

# RASPBERRY CHEESECAKE BARS

lta Henderson of Hopkins, Minnesota, layers a cheesecake filling over an almond crust, then adds a raspberry topper to make these first-rate bars. (Pictured on page 11.)

1¼ cups all-purpose flour
½ cup packed brown sugar
½ cup finely chopped almonds
½ cup butter-flavored shortening or regular shortening
2 8-ounce packages cream cheese, softened

⅔ cup sugar
2 eggs
¾ teaspoon almond extract
1 cup seedless raspberry preserves or other preserves or jam
½ cup flaked coconut
½ cup sliced almonds

1 In a mixing bowl, combine the flour, brown sugar and the ½ cup finely chopped almonds. Using a pastry blender, cut in shortening till mixture resembles fine crumbs. Set aside ½ *cup* for topping.

2 For crust, press the remaining crumb mixture into the bottom of a 13×9×2-inch baking pan. Bake in a 350° oven for 12 to 15 minutes or till the edges are golden brown.

3 Meanwhile, in another mixing bowl, beat the cream cheese, sugar, eggs and almond extract till smooth. Spread over the hot crust. Return to oven and bake for 15 minutes.

4 Spread preserves over cream cheese mixture. In a small bowl, combine the reserved crumb mixture, coconut and the ½ cup sliced almonds. Sprinkle over preserves. Return to oven and bake for 15 minutes more. Cool in pan on a wire rack. Refrigerate for 3 hours before cutting into bars. Store the cheesecake bars in the refrigerator. Makes 32 bars.

# CHOCOLATE THUMBPRINTS

or added taste appeal, Jan Kensler of Omaha, Nebraska, stirs melted chocolate into the traditional thumbprint cookie dough. Fill the centers with either the Thumbprint Frosting or Marble Frosting.

½ cup butter, softened
¾ cup sugar
⅛ teaspoon salt
1 egg
1 ounce unsweetened chocolate, melted and cooled
½ teaspoon vanilla

1 cup all-purpose flour
1 tablespoon water
1 cup finely chopped walnuts
Thumbprint Frosting or Marble Frosting (recipes follow)

1 In a large mixing bowl, beat together the butter, sugar and salt with an electric mixer till light and fluffy. Separate egg; set the white aside. Add the yolk, melted chocolate and vanilla to the butter mixture; beat well.

2 Add the flour. Beat or stir till combined. Roll dough into 1-inch balls. Mix egg white with the water. Dip balls first into egg white mixture, then into nuts.

3 Place on greased cookie sheets. Press centers with your thumb to make a shallow indent in each cookie. Bake in a 350° oven for 10 to 12 minutes or till edges are set. Cool 1 minute. Transfer cookies to wire racks; cool.

4 Prepare Thumbprint Frosting or Marble Frosting. Fill cookie centers. Makes about 36 cookies.

**Thumbprint Frosting:** Combine 1 cup sifted *powdered sugar* and enough *milk* (1 to 2 tablespoons) to make a mixture of spooning consistency. If you like, tint with *food coloring*.

**Marble Frosting:** In a small mixing bowl, beat 3 tablespoons *butter* with an electric mixer till light and fluffy. Gradually add about 1 cup sifted *powdered sugar*, beating well. Beat in 2 tablespoons *milk* and ¾ teaspoon *vanilla*. Gradually beat in 1¼ to 1½ cups sifted *powdered sugar* to make a frosting of piping consistency. Tint *half* of the frosting with *food coloring*. Place equal parts plain and colored frosting in a decorating bag fitted with a ¼-inch star tip. Fill centers of cookies.

# DOUBLE CHERRY PIE

**H**eartland cherry lovers can enjoy this delectable pie year-round because it's made with canned tart cherries and cherry pie filling. The chocolate-oat crust gives it a homespun touch.

½ cup miniature semisweet chocolate pieces
5 tablespoons butter
¾ cup rolled oats
¾ cup all-purpose flour
¼ cup packed brown sugar
1 16-ounce can reduced-calorie cherry pie filling
1 16-ounce can pitted tart red cherries (water-packed), drained

¼ teaspoon almond extract
½ cup all-purpose flour
2 tablespoons packed brown sugar
2 tablespoons rolled oats
3 tablespoons butter, softened
¼ cup miniature semisweet chocolate pieces

**1** Grease a 10-inch pie plate. Set aside. For crust, in a medium saucepan, melt the ½ cup chocolate pieces and 5 tablespoons butter. Remove from heat; stir in the ¾ cup oats, ¾ cup flour and ¼ cup brown sugar. Press onto bottom and sides of prepared pie plate to form a firm, even crust. Bake in a 350° oven for 10 minutes.

**2** Meanwhile, for filling, in a medium mixing bowl, combine pie filling, cherries and almond extract. Pour into the baked crust.

**3** For topping, in a small mixing bowl, stir together the ½ cup flour, 2 tablespoons brown sugar and 2 tablespoons oats. Cut in the 3 tablespoons butter till mixture resembles coarse crumbs. Stir in the ¼ cup chocolate pieces. Sprinkle over cherry filling. Bake in 350° oven for 35 minutes. Cool on a wire rack. Makes 10 servings.

# SOUR CREAM-RHUBARB PIE

**B**ecky Harms of Wichita, Kansas, took a favorite custard-apple pie recipe and adapted it for summer's abundant rhubarb. The pie is her husband's favorite dessert. Becky, who usually isn't fond of rhubarb, likes it too.

Single-Crust Pastry (recipe page 21)
1 cup light dairy sour cream
2 eggs
1½ cups sugar
2 tablespoons all-purpose flour

1 teaspoon vanilla
¼ teaspoon salt
3 cups chopped fresh or frozen rhubarb, thawed
¼ cup packed brown sugar
¼ cup all-purpose flour
3 tablespoons butter

**1** Prepare Single-Crust Pastry as directed, except trim pastry ¾ inch beyond edge of pie plate. Fold pastry under and flute the edge. Set aside.

**2** For filling, in a large mixing bowl, stir together sour cream and eggs. Stir in sugar, the 2 tablespoons flour, vanilla and salt. Stir in the chopped rhubarb.

**3** Pour the filling into the prepared pastry shell. Cover the pie with foil. Bake in a 450° oven for 15 minutes. Reduce the oven temperature to 350° and bake for 20 minutes more.

**4** Meanwhile, in a small mixing bowl, stir together the brown sugar and ¼ cup flour. Using a pastry blender, cut in butter till mixture resembles coarse crumbs. Sprinkle mixture over rhubarb filling.

**5** Bake, uncovered, for 20 to 25 minutes more or till filling is set. Cool on a wire rack. Store, covered, in the refrigerator. Makes 8 servings.

DOUBLE CHERRY PIE

# BLACKBERRY-PECAN STREUSEL PIE

 onnie Moore of Medway, Ohio, precooks the juicy, tart blackberry filling before pouring it into the piecrust. When she bakes this pie, the streusel topping becomes a crunchy sugar-pecan crown.

**Single-Crust Pastry (recipe page 21)**
**4 cups fresh or frozen unsweetened blackberries**
**1 cup sugar**
**⅓ cup quick-cooking tapioca**
**1 teaspoon ground cinnamon**
**Pecan Streusel Topping (recipe follows)**

1 Prepare Single-Crust Pastry as directed. Line the pastry with a double thickness of heavy foil. Bake in a 450° oven for 8 minutes. Remove the foil. Bake for 4 to 5 minutes more or till crust is golden. Reduce the oven temperature to 375°.

2 Meanwhile, in a medium saucepan, combine the blackberries, sugar, tapioca and cinnamon. Cook and stir over medium heat till mixture starts to bubble. Reduce heat and simmer the berry filling, uncovered, for 10 minutes, stirring the mixture frequently.

3 Pour the berry filling into the prepared pastry shell. Top with the Pecan Streusel Topping.

4 Bake the pie in the 375° oven for 25 to 30 minutes or till crust and topping are golden brown. Makes 6 to 8 servings.

**Pecan Streusel Topping:** In a medium bowl, combine ½ cup *all-purpose flour* and ¼ cup *sugar*. Using a pastry blender, cut in ¼ cup cold *butter* till the pieces are the size of small peas. Stir in ¼ cup finely chopped *pecans*.

---

# SHOO-FLY PIE

 ave room for pie when dining out in Amish country. Serving specialty pies upholds a tradition in the Amish communities. This old-fashioned molasses dessert comes from Amish Acres in Nappanee, Indiana.

**Single-Crust Pastry (recipe page 21)**
**1¼ cups all-purpose flour**
**½ cup packed brown sugar**
**½ teaspoon ground cinnamon**
**¼ teaspoon salt**
**3 tablespoons cooking oil**
**¾ cup boiling water**
**½ teaspoon baking soda**
**½ cup dark corn syrup**
**¼ cup light-flavored molasses**
**1 beaten egg**

1 Prepare Single-Crust Pastry as directed. Set aside.

2 In a small bowl, combine the flour, brown sugar, cinnamon and salt. Mix in oil till mixture is crumbly. Set aside.

3 In another mixing bowl, combine the boiling water and baking soda. Stir in the corn syrup and molasses. Let the mixture cool till just warm. Beat in the egg.

4 Sprinkle *½ cup* of the flour mixture over the bottom of the prepared pastry shell. Carefully pour in the molasses mixture. Sprinkle remaining flour mixture evenly over pie.

5 Bake in a 375° oven for 25 to 30 minutes or till set. Cool on a wire rack. Store pie, covered, in the refrigerator. Makes 8 servings.

# PUMPKIN-PECAN CRUMBLE PIE

ven if you normally pass up dessert, you'll probably succumb to temptation if you dine at any of the numerous smorgasbords found in the Heartland. They often feature irresistible pies such as this one.

**Single-Crust Pastry**
  **(recipe below)**
**1 16-ounce can pumpkin**
**⅔ cup sugar**
**2 teaspoons pumpkin pie**
  **spice**

**3 eggs**
**1 5-ounce can (⅔ cup)**
  **evaporated milk**
**½ cup milk**
  **Pecan Crumble Topping**
  **(recipe follows)**

**1** Prepare Single-Crust Pastry as directed. Set aside.

**2** For filling, in a mixing bowl, combine pumpkin, sugar and spice. Add the eggs and beat lightly. Gradually beat in the evaporated milk and milk.

**3** Pour the filling into the crust. Cover the edge of the pie with foil to prevent overbrowning. Bake in a 375° oven for 25 minutes.

**4** Meanwhile, prepare Pecan Crumble Topping. Remove foil from pie. Sprinkle topping over filling.

**5** Return pie to oven. Bake about 25 minutes more or till a knife inserted near the center comes out clean. Cool on wire rack. Store, covered, in the refrigerator. Makes 8 servings.

**Pecan Crumble Topping:** In a medium bowl, combine ½ cup *all-purpose flour*, ½ cup chopped *pecans*, ¼ cup packed *brown sugar* and 3 tablespoons softened *butter*.

---

# SINGLE-CRUST PASTRY

any a Heartland cook will tell you that one of the secrets to a scrumptious pie is the crust. With this easy recipe, your piecrusts will turn out tender and flaky every time.

**1¼ cups all-purpose flour**
**¼ teaspoon salt**
**⅓ cup shortening or lard**

**3 to 4 tablespoons cold**
  **water**

**1** In a mixing bowl, stir together the flour and salt. Using a pastry blender, cut in shortening till pieces are the size of small peas.

**2** Sprinkle *1 tablespoon* of the water over part of the flour mixture; gently toss with a fork. Push to sides of bowl. Repeat with remaining water till all is moistened. Form dough into a ball.

**3** On a lightly floured surface, flatten the dough with your hands. Roll dough from center to edges, forming a circle about 12 inches in diameter. Wrap pastry around rolling pin. Unroll onto a 9-inch pie plate. Ease the pastry into the pie plate, being careful not to stretch the pastry as you move it.

**4** Trim pastry to ½ inch beyond edge of pie plate and fold under the extra pastry. Finish the crust as you like, making a fluted, rope-shaped or scalloped edge. Don't prick pastry. Fill and bake pastry as directed in individual recipes.

# U.S.S. MISSOURI BUTTERMILK PIE

This pie comes from Barbara Wagner of Columbia, Missouri. She began making the recipe 27 years ago when her husband, Al, brought it home from the Navy. The pie is named after the battleship Missouri.

**Single-Crust Pastry
(recipe page 21)**
**2 cups sugar**
**½ cup butter, softened**
**3 eggs**

**3 tablespoons all-purpose
flour**
**¼ teaspoon salt**
**1 cup buttermilk**
**½ cup chopped pecans,
toasted***

**1** Prepare Single-Crust Pastry as directed, except trim pastry ¾ inch beyond edge of pie plate. Fold pastry under and flute the edge. Set aside.

**2** In a large mixing bowl, gradually beat the sugar into the softened butter with an electric mixer, beating till mixture is well combined. Beat in the eggs, one at a time, beating well after each addition.

**3** Combine flour and salt. Gradually add the flour mixture to the butter mixture, beating till well combined. Beat in the buttermilk till well combined. Pour the buttermilk mixture into the prepared pastry shell. Sprinkle the pecans over mixture.

**4** Bake the pie in a 300° oven for 75 to 80 minutes or till set. Cool on wire rack. Store pie in the refrigerator. Serves 8.

**\*Note:** To toast the chopped pecans, spread them evenly in a shallow baking pan. Bake the pecans in a 350° oven for 5 to 10 minutes or till browned, stirring the nuts once or twice during baking.

# CHEESY APPLE PIE

With an apple orchard just down the road, it makes sense that Sharon Clifton, who lives on a dairy farm outside Purdy, Missouri, would mix apples and cheese for this family-favorite pie.

**1 cup all-purpose flour**
**¼ teaspoon salt**
**⅓ cup butter-flavored
shortening or regular
shortening**
**½ cup finely shredded
cheddar cheese**
**3 to 4 tablespoons cold
water**

**5 cups thinly sliced, peeled
cooking apples**
**1 cup sugar**
**¼ cup all-purpose flour**
**1 teaspoon ground
cinnamon**
**¼ teaspoon salt**
**Cheddar Crunch Topping
(recipe follows)**

**1** In a mixing bowl, stir together the 1 cup flour and ¼ teaspoon salt. Using a pastry blender, cut in the shortening till pieces are the size of small peas. Stir in cheese. Sprinkle *1 tablespoon* of the water over part of the mixture; gently toss with a fork. Repeat with remaining water till all is moistened. Form into a ball.

**2** On a floured surface, roll out pastry to a 12-inch circle. Ease into 9-inch pie plate. Trim to ½ inch beyond edge of plate; fold pastry under. Flute edge.

**3** Combine apples, sugar, the ¼ cup flour, cinnamon and ¼ teaspoon salt. Spoon into pastry shell.

**4** Sprinkle Cheddar Crunch Topping over filling. Cover edge with foil. Bake in a 375° oven for 25 minutes. Remove foil. Bake for 20 to 25 minutes more or till top is golden and fruit is tender. Serves 8.

**Cheddar Crunch Topping:** In a medium bowl, stir together ¾ cup *sugar*, ¾ cup *all-purpose flour* and ¼ teaspoon *salt*. Using a pastry blender, cut in ⅓ cup *butter* till mixture is crumbly. Gently stir in 1 cup finely shredded *cheddar cheese* (4 ounces).

# CHEESY APPLE PIE

# SOUR CREAM-CHOCOLATE CAKE

The easy no-cook fudgelike frosting adds to this moist sour cream cake's rich chocolate flavor. The decadent treat is a favorite at the Mount Marty Oktoberfest in Yankton, South Dakota.

2 cups sifted cake flour or
    1¾ cups all-purpose
    flour
1 teaspoon baking powder
½ teaspoon baking soda
½ teaspoon salt
1¼ cups sugar
½ cup shortening
2 eggs

1 teaspoon vanilla
3 ounces unsweetened
    chocolate, melted and
    cooled
⅔ cup dairy sour cream
¾ cup milk
    No-Cook Fudge Frosting
    (recipe follows)
1 teaspoon cognac or
    brandy (optional)

1. Grease and flour two 8×1½-inch round baking pans. In a medium bowl, combine flour, baking powder, baking soda and salt. Set aside.

2. In a large mixing bowl, beat sugar and shortening with electric mixer till combined. Add eggs and vanilla; beat till light. Stir in melted chocolate and sour cream. Add flour mixture and milk alternately to chocolate mixture, beating after each addition till just combined. Pour into prepared pans.

3. Bake in a 350° oven about 30 minutes or till tops spring back when lightly touched. Cool on wire racks for 10 minutes. Remove from pans; cool on racks.

4. Once the cakes are cooled, prepare No-Cook Fudge Frosting. (If you like, stir cognac or brandy into ½ cup of the cooled frosting.) Place one cake layer on cake plate. Spread ½ cup of the frosting (or, if using, the ½ cup cognac-flavored frosting) over top of one layer. Place other layer on top. Frost top and sides with remaining frosting. Makes 12 servings.

**No-Cook Fudge Frosting:** In a large mixing bowl, stir together 4¾ cups sifted *powdered sugar* and ½ cup *unsweetened cocoa powder*. Add ½ cup *butter*, softened; ⅓ cup *boiling water*; and 1 teaspoon *vanilla*. Beat with an electric mixer on low speed till combined. Beat for 1 minute on medium speed. Cover and cool for 20 to 30 minutes or till of spreading consistency.

---

# PERFECT PEACH CAKE

Yes, it is—perfect that is—especially served warm from the oven. This moist cake comes from Helen Lemon of Lemon Creek Fruit Farms, Vineyards and Winery in Berrien Springs, Michigan.

1½ cups packed brown sugar
⅔ cup butter, softened
2 eggs
2 cups all-purpose flour
1 teaspoon baking soda
⅛ teaspoon salt
1 cup buttermilk or sour
    milk*

4 medium peaches, peeled
    and chopped, or 3 cups
    frozen unsweetened
    peach slices, thawed
    and chopped
¼ cup sugar
1 teaspoon ground
    cinnamon

1. Grease and flour a 13×9×2-inch baking pan. Set aside. In a large bowl, beat brown sugar and butter with electric mixer till light and fluffy. Beat in eggs.

2. In a medium bowl, stir together flour, baking soda and salt. Add flour mixture and buttermilk or sour milk alternately to the creamed mixture, beating well after each addition. Stir in peaches by hand.

3. Pour batter into prepared pan. In a bowl, combine sugar and cinnamon. Sprinkle over top of batter.

4. Bake in a 350° oven about 40 minutes or till a wooden toothpick inserted near the center comes out clean. Serve warm. Makes 12 servings.

**\*Note:** To make sour milk, place 1 tablespoon *lemon juice* in a glass measuring cup. Pour in enough *milk* to make 1 cup liquid. Stir and let stand for 5 minutes.

# GINGER-FRESH GINGERBREAD

**T**his molasses gingerbread with a sweet, sugary crust gets its heavenly taste from fresh gingerroot. At The Flower Patch bed-and-breakfast in Arcola, Illinois, Lynne Harshbarger tops the cake with whipped cream.

2¼ cups all-purpose flour
1 teaspoon baking soda
1 teaspoon ground
    cinnamon
½ teaspoon salt
½ cup shortening
2 tablespoons sugar
1 egg

1 cup dark-flavored
    molasses
1 cup boiling water
1 teaspoon grated fresh
    gingerroot
    Sifted powdered sugar
    Sweetened whipped
    cream (optional)

**1** Grease and flour a 9×1½-inch round baking pan or a 9×9×2-inch baking pan. In a bowl, stir together the flour, baking soda, cinnamon and salt. Set aside.

**2** In a large mixing bowl, beat together the shortening, sugar and egg. Beat in molasses and boiling water. Gradually beat in the flour mixture. Stir in the grated gingerroot.

**3** Turn the batter into prepared pan. Bake in a 325° oven for 40 to 45 minutes or till a wooden toothpick inserted in the center comes out clean.

**4** Cool on a wire rack for 10 minutes. Turn out onto a serving plate and sprinkle with powdered sugar. If you like, serve warm with whipped cream. Serves 12.

**Note:** For a decorative powdered sugar top, place a paper doily over the gingerbread and sprinkle with powdered sugar. Then, carefully remove the doily.

# LINDA'S LEMONY PRAIRIE CAKE

**L**inda McDiffett, who lives on a 3,200-acre spread near Alta Vista, Kansas, bakes this moist, citrus-flavored cake to serve at parties or special occasions. The secret ingredient is lemon-lime soda pop.

1½ cups butter
3 cups sugar
5 eggs
3 cups all-purpose flour

¾ cup lemon-lime
    carbonated beverage
2 tablespoons lemon
    extract

**1** Grease and lightly flour a 10-inch fluted tube pan. Set aside. In a large mixing bowl, beat butter and sugar together till light and fluffy. Add eggs, one at a time, beating well after each addition.

**2** Beat in flour, *1 cup* at a time. Beat in lemon-lime carbonated beverage and lemon extract. Pour into prepared pan.

**3** Bake in 350° oven for 60 to 65 minutes or till a wooden toothpick inserted near the center comes out clean. Cool on a wire rack for 10 minutes. Loosen sides of cake; remove from pan. Cool on wire rack. Makes 12 servings.

# MARY TODD LINCOLN'S CINNAMON CAKE

 braham Lincoln declared his devotion to his wife, Mary, with an inscription inside her wedding band: "Love Is Eternal." Mary showed her affection for her husband by making his favorite desserts, such as this cake.

1 cup currants or raisins
¼ cup brandy or orange juice
1 package active dry yeast
1¼ cups warm milk (105° to 115°)
1 tablespoon sugar
1 cup all-purpose flour
2¾ cups all-purpose flour
1¼ teaspoons ground cinnamon

¾ teaspoon ground mace
½ teaspoon salt
1 cup sugar
¾ cup butter
1 egg
1 teaspoon grated lemon peel
2 teaspoons lemon juice
Orange Glaze (recipe follows)

1 In a jar, combine currants and brandy or orange juice. Cover tightly. Let stand overnight.

2 In a medium bowl, combine the yeast, milk and the 1 tablespoon sugar. Let stand till mixture is bubbly. By hand, beat in the 1 cup flour till smooth. Cover and let rise in a warm place till doubled (about 45 minutes).

3 In a bowl, mix the 2¾ cups flour, cinnamon, mace and salt. Drain currants; reserve liquid. Grease a 10-inch fluted tube pan or 10-inch tube pan. Set aside.

4 In a large bowl, beat the 1 cup sugar and butter with electric mixer till very light. Add egg; beat till light. Beat in lemon peel, lemon juice and reserved liquid. Beat in yeast mixture. By hand, stir in drained currants. Stir in flour mixture till combined. Turn batter into pan. Cover; let rise in a warm place 1 hour.

5 Bake in a 350° oven 40 to 45 minutes or till wooden toothpick inserted near center comes out clean. Cool on a wire rack 10 minutes. Remove from pan. Cool on a rack. Drizzle with Orange Glaze. Serves 12.

**Orange Glaze:** In a bowl, stir together 1 cup sifted *powdered sugar* and 2 tablespoons *orange juice* till the mixture is smooth and drizzles easily.

# LIGHTER CHOCOLATE FUDGE CAKE

T his scrumptious chocolate cake is a lighter version of a favorite recipe of Jean Gehrt's of Waupaca, Wisconsin. It uses reduced-calorie cake mix, egg product and applesauce instead of oil.

Nonstick spray coating
1 package 2-layer-size reduced-fat devil's food cake mix
1 4-serving-size package instant chocolate fudge pudding mix
1¼ cups water
1 8-ounce carton refrigerated or frozen egg product, thawed

¼ cup applesauce
¼ cup miniature semisweet chocolate pieces
¼ cup chopped walnuts
Frozen light whipped dessert topping, thawed, or fat-free vanilla ice cream (optional)

1 Spray a 13×9×2-inch baking pan or 10-inch fluted tube pan with nonstick coating. Set aside. In a large mixing bowl, stir together the cake mix and pudding mix. Add the water, egg product and applesauce. Beat with an electric mixer on low speed till combined. Beat on medium speed for 2 minutes.

2 Spread the cake batter in prepared pan. Sprinkle the chocolate pieces over the cake batter, then sprinkle with walnuts.

3 If using a 13×9×2-inch pan, bake in a 350° oven about 35 minutes or till a wooden toothpick inserted near the center comes out clean. Cool cake completely on a wire rack. If using a 10-inch tube pan, bake cake in a 350° oven for 45 minutes. Cool cake 15 minutes on wire rack; remove cake from fluted tube pan and cool completely. If you like, serve with whipped dessert topping or fat-free ice cream. Makes 15 servings.

MARY TODD
LINCOLN'S
CINNAMON CAKE

# BUTTERMILK-COCONUT CAKE

uscious cakes reign supreme at many Midwestern smorgasbord-style restaurants. Here's a coconut-covered showstopper that will make your own home-cooked buffet shine. It's a favorite among many Midwesterners.

| | |
|---|---|
| **2 cups all-purpose flour** | **5 egg whites** |
| **1½ teaspoons baking powder** | **1 cup buttermilk or sour milk*** |
| **¼ teaspoon baking soda** | |
| **½ cup shortening** | **Butter Frosting (recipe follows)** |
| **¼ cup butter** | |
| **1½ cups sugar** | **1 cup flaked coconut (toasted, if you like)** |
| **1 teaspoon vanilla** | |

**1** Grease and flour two 8×1½-inch or two 9×1½-inch round baking pans. Set aside. In a medium mixing bowl, stir together the flour, baking powder and baking soda.

**2** In a mixing bowl, beat the shortening and butter with an electric mixer about 30 seconds or till softened. Add the sugar and vanilla; beat till fluffy. Add the egg whites; beat till smooth (about 2 minutes).

**3** Add flour mixture and buttermilk or sour milk alternately to beaten mixture, beating on low speed after each addition till mixture is just combined.

**4** Turn batter into prepared pans. Bake in a 375° oven for 25 to 30 minutes or till a wooden toothpick inserted near the centers comes out clean.

**5** Cool on wire racks for 10 minutes. Remove from pans; cool completely on wire racks.

**6** Spread Butter Frosting between layers and over top and sides. Sprinkle top and sides with coconut. Makes 12 servings.

**Butter Frosting:** In a small mixing bowl, beat ½ cup *butter* till light. Gradually add 3 cups sifted *powdered sugar*, beating well. Beat in ⅓ cup *milk* and 2 teaspoons *vanilla*. Gradually beat in 3¾ to 4 cups sifted *powdered sugar* to make a spreadable frosting. Makes 3 cups.

***Note:** To make sour milk, place 1 tablespoon *lemon juice* in a glass measuring cup. Pour in enough *milk* to make 1 cup liquid. Stir and let stand for 5 minutes.

---

# SCHLÖEGEL'S APPLE CAKE

t Schlöegel's Bay View Restaurant in Menominee, Michigan, waitresses generously ladle warm lemon sauce over this freshly baked apple cake. Serve the cake in small bowls to ensure a fair share of the satiny sauce.

| | |
|---|---|
| **2 cups sugar** | **4 cups diced, peeled apples** |
| **1 cup butter, softened** | **1 cup packed brown sugar** |
| **4 eggs** | **1 tablespoon ground cinnamon** |
| **2 teaspoons vanilla** | |
| **2 cups all-purpose flour** | **½ teaspoon ground nutmeg** |
| **2 teaspoons baking powder** | **Lemon Sauce (recipe follows)** |
| **½ teaspoon salt** | |

**1** Grease a 13×9×2-inch baking pan. Set aside. In a large bowl, beat together sugar, butter, eggs and vanilla with an electric mixer till well combined.

**2** Add flour, baking powder and salt. Beat till just combined. Spread *half* the batter in prepared pan. In another bowl, combine the apples, brown sugar, cinnamon and nutmeg. Spread the mixture over the batter in pan. Dollop the remaining batter over apples.

**3** Bake in a 350° oven about 60 minutes or till a wooden toothpick inserted in the center comes out clean. Cool in pan on wire rack for 30 minutes. Serve warm with warm Lemon Sauce. Makes 12 servings.

**Lemon Sauce:** In a medium saucepan, combine 1 cup *sugar*, 3 tablespoons *cornstarch*, ¼ teaspoon *ground nutmeg* and ¼ teaspoon *salt*. Stir in 2½ cups *water*. Cook and stir till mixture is thickened and bubbly. Cook and stir for 2 minutes more. Stir in 6 tablespoons *butter*, 1 teaspoon grated *lemon peel* and ¼ cup *lemon juice*. Makes 3½ cups.

# TRUDIE'S DUTCH APPLE CAKE

emon in the buttery crust, as well as in the creamy filling, accents the flavor of this homey apple dessert from Trudie Seybold, owner of the Forest View Gardens restaurant in Cincinnati, Ohio.

⅔ cup butter
½ cup sugar
1 teaspoon finely shredded lemon peel
2 cups all-purpose flour
3 tablespoons butter
¾ cup coarsely crushed cornflakes
1 teaspoon sugar
2 eggs
¼ cup sugar

1 8-ounce carton dairy sour cream
½ teaspoon finely shredded lemon peel
5½ cups sliced, peeled apples (5 to 6 medium)
½ cup sugar
1 teaspoon ground cinnamon
1 teaspoon finely shredded lemon peel

**1** For crust, in a medium bowl, beat the ⅔ cup butter with an electric mixer about 30 seconds or till softened. Add the ½ cup sugar and 1 teaspoon lemon peel; beat till combined. Beat in flour till crumbly. Press into the bottom of an ungreased 13×9×2-inch baking pan. Bake in a 350° oven for 15 to 18 minutes or till edges are light brown. Remove from oven.

**2** In a skillet, melt the 3 tablespoons butter. Add cornflakes and the 1 teaspoon sugar. Cook and stir over medium heat for 1 to 2 minutes or till cornflakes are lightly browned. Remove from heat. Set aside.

**3** In a medium mixing bowl, beat eggs till foamy. Add the ¼ cup sugar; beat till thick and lemon-colored (about 5 minutes). Fold in the sour cream and the ½ teaspoon lemon peel.

**4** In a large saucepan, combine the apples and a small amount of *water*. Bring to boiling; reduce heat. Simmer, covered, for 3 minutes or till apples are just tender. Drain well. Cool slightly.

**5** In a small bowl, combine the ⅓ cup sugar, the cinnamon and 1 teaspoon lemon peel. Toss with the apple slices. Arrange coated slices over baked crust. Pour the sour cream mixture evenly over the apples. Sprinkle with the cornflake mixture.

**6** Bake in a 350° oven about 35 minutes or till cornflake mixture is golden brown. Cool slightly. Cut into squares. Makes 12 servings.

## Is It Done Yet?

The secret to moist, tender cakes is knowing when to take them out of the oven. For perfectly baked cakes, remember these two rules of thumb:

♦ To test a layer cake for doneness, insert a wooden toothpick into the cake near the center. The toothpick should come out clean with no batter clinging to it. If it is not clean, return the cake to the oven and bake it a few minutes longer. Then, using a clean toothpick, test the cake again in another spot near the center.

♦ To test an angel food, sponge or chiffon cake, touch the top lightly. If the top springs back, the cake is done.

# ST. LOUIS GOOEY BUTTER CAKE

This cake was shared by Rozanek's Bakery of St. Louis. The recipe—a coffee cake with a thin, rich, doughy bottom layer—was accidentally created in the '30s by a baker who used the wrong proportion of ingredients.

1 cup all-purpose flour
3 tablespoons sugar
⅓ cup butter
1¼ cups sugar
¾ cup butter

¼ cup light corn syrup
1 egg
1 cup all-purpose flour
⅔ cup evaporated milk
Sifted powdered sugar
(optional)

**1** In a mixing bowl, combine the 1 cup flour and 3 tablespoons sugar. Using a pastry blender, cut in the ⅓ cup butter till mixture resembles fine crumbs and starts to cling. Pat into the bottom of an ungreased 9×9×2-inch baking pan.

**2** For filling, in a mixing bowl, beat the 1¼ cups sugar and ¾ cup butter till thoroughly combined. Beat in the corn syrup and egg till just combined.

**3** Add the 1 cup flour and evaporated milk alternately to the filling, beating till just combined (batter will appear slightly curdled).

**4** Pour into crust-lined baking pan. Bake in a 350° oven about 35 minutes or till cake is nearly firm when you shake it. Cool in pan on wire rack. Remove from pan onto serving plate. If you like, sprinkle with powdered sugar. Makes 9 servings.

# SHOWY PINEAPPLE CAKE

The old-fashioned flavor of pineapple upside-down cake is fondly remembered in this delicious, easy-to-make version. Popular in the 1920s, it's a home-style dessert that has withstood the test of time.

Nonstick spray coating
1 tablespoon butter
¼ cup packed brown sugar
2 tablespoons light corn
syrup
1 8-ounce can pineapple
slices (juice-packed),
drained and halved

4 maraschino cherries,
halved
1 cup all-purpose flour
1 teaspoon baking powder
2 egg whites
1 egg
¾ cup sugar
½ cup milk
2 tablespoons butter

**1** Spray a 9×1½-inch round baking pan with nonstick coating. Melt the 1 tablespoon butter in the pan by placing the pan in the oven for 5 minutes while the oven preheats to 350°. Remove pan from oven. Stir brown sugar and corn syrup into melted butter. Spread evenly in pan. Arrange pineapple and cherries in pan over butter mixture. Set aside.

**2** In a small bowl, combine flour and baking powder. In a medium mixing bowl, beat egg whites and egg with an electric mixer on high speed for 4 minutes. Gradually add the sugar, beating till light and fluffy. Add flour mixture; beat till just combined.

**3** In a small saucepan, cook and stir the milk and the 2 tablespoons butter over medium heat till butter melts. Add to the batter, beating till combined. Pour into pan over pineapple.

**4** Bake in a 350° oven for 30 to 35 minutes or till a wooden toothpick inserted in center of cake comes out clean. Cool on wire rack for 5 minutes. Loosen the sides and invert the cake onto a serving plate. Serve warm. Makes 8 servings.

# JUMBO APPLE DUMPLINGS

Pat Maycock of Waverly, Missouri, continues her mother's tradition of baking these extra-large apple dumplings for family gatherings. A spiced syrup bakes along with the dumplings, forming a sauce to spoon over each serving.

2 cups all-purpose flour
2 teaspoons baking powder
1 teaspoon salt
⅔ cup shortening
⅓ to ½ cup milk
6 medium cooking apples, peeled and cored (about 5 ounces each)
1 cup sugar
1¼ teaspoons ground cinnamon

2 tablespoons butter
1½ cups sugar
1½ cups water
¼ teaspoon ground cinnamon
¼ teaspoon ground nutmeg
3 tablespoons butter
Sugared cranberries* (optional)
Ice cream or cream

**1** In a mixing bowl, combine the flour, baking powder and salt. Using a pastry blender, cut in the shortening till mixture is about the size of small peas.

**2** Sprinkle *1 tablespoon* of the milk over part of mixture; toss with a fork. Push mixture to sides of bowl. Repeat with the remaining milk till all is moistened. Divide dough into 6 portions; shape into balls. Cover and set aside.

**3** On a lightly floured surface, roll each ball to an 8-inch circle; trim to a 7½-inch circle. (If you like, reserve trimmings for pastry leaves.) Place an apple in the center of each circle.

**4** Mix the 1 cup sugar and 1¼ teaspoons cinnamon. Divide mixture among the apples, spooning it into the center of each apple. Top each apple with 1 teaspoon of the butter.

**5** Moisten the edges of pastry with some *water*. Bring dough up around each apple to form a bundle, pressing the edges together at the top to seal.

**6** If you like, roll out dough trimmings; cut into leaf shapes. Brush tops of dumplings with some *water*; arrange leaves on top of each dumpling, pressing into place. Lightly grease a 3-quart rectangular baking dish. Place apple dumplings in prepared dish.

**7** For syrup, in a saucepan, combine the 1½ cups sugar, 1½ cups water, ¼ teaspoon cinnamon and the nutmeg. Bring to boiling. Remove from heat; stir in the 3 tablespoons butter. Pour over apples.

**8** Bake in a 375° oven for 35 to 40 minutes or till apples are tender and pastry is browned. If you like, garnish with cranberries. Serve warm with ice cream or cream. Makes 6 dumplings.

**\*Note:** To make sugared cranberries, dip them in *refrigerated egg product*. Then, roll in *sugar*.

# RASPBERRY-ORANGE CRUMBLE

The Gilded Vine Cooking School at Firelands Winery in Sandusky, Ohio, contributed its version of this traditional dessert, which sets itself apart with its distinctive orange liqueur accent.

4 cups fresh red raspberries or frozen raspberries, thawed
½ to ¾ cup sugar
¼ cup triple sec or orange juice

1 cup all-purpose flour
½ cup packed light brown sugar
¼ teaspoon ground nutmeg
¼ cup butter, cut up
Cream or ice cream

**1** Butter a 2-quart square (8×8×2-inch) baking dish. In a large bowl, toss together raspberries, sugar and triple sec or orange juice. Spoon into prepared dish.

**2** In a food processor bowl, combine the flour, brown sugar and nutmeg. Add the butter. Cover and process till mixture resembles fine crumbs. (Or, in a medium mixing bowl, combine the flour, brown sugar and nutmeg. Using a pastry blender, cut in the butter till mixture resembles fine crumbs.) Spoon over the raspberries in dish.

**3** Bake in a 375° oven for 30 to 35 minutes or till golden brown and bubbles cover entire surface. Serve warm with cream or ice cream. Makes 6 servings.

# CINNAMON BREAD PUDDING WITH BUTTER SAUCE

 sing cubed cinnamon bread or cinnamon rolls makes this bread pudding easy as well as delicious. The cooks at Ruttger's Sugar Lake Lodge near Grand Rapids, Minnesota, top it with the warm Butter Sauce.

6 eggs
2 cups milk
1¾ cups half-and-half or light
    cream
1 cup sugar
2 teaspoons vanilla

6 cups cubed cinnamon
    bread or cinnamon rolls
    without icing (about
    1 pound)
Butter Sauce (recipe
    follows)

1 For pudding, in a large mixing bowl, beat eggs with a wire whisk. Beat in milk, half-and-half, sugar and vanilla till combined. Stir in the cinnamon bread.

2 Grease a 2-quart rectangular (12×7½×2-inch) baking dish. Add bread mixture, spreading evenly.

3 Bake in a 325° oven for 55 to 60 minutes or till top is puffed and a knife inserted near the center comes out clean. Serve warm with warm Butter Sauce. Makes 8 to 10 servings.

**Butter Sauce:** In a small saucepan, heat ½ cup packed *brown sugar* and ¼ cup *butter* till butter melts. Carefully add ⅓ cup *light corn syrup* and ¼ cup *half-and-half* or *light cream*. Cook, stirring constantly, over medium-low heat for 1 to 2 minutes or till sugar is dissolved and mixture is smooth. Makes about 1 cup.

**Note:** If the Butter Sauce separates while standing, just stir the sauce briskly till it's blended again.

## Seconds, Please

To make the leftovers from bread pudding taste just as good the second time around, transfer the pudding to a smaller casserole or ovenproof dish. Transfer any leftover sauce to a small bowl. Cover both containers and refrigerate for up to 2 days. To reheat the pudding, cover the casserole or dish with the casserole lid or foil. Bake in a 350° oven till the center is warm. To reheat the sauce, transfer it to a small saucepan. Heat over medium-low heat, stirring constantly, till the sugar is dissolved and the mixture is smooth.

# FAMILY-FAVORITE PEACH-PECAN COBBLER

Carlene Smith of Rockford, Illinois, puts a new twist on a seasonal favorite by topping summer-best peaches with sweet swirls of pecan-studded biscuits. A splash of cream or a scoop of ice cream is heavenly.

¾ cup sugar
1 tablespoon cornstarch
½ teaspoon ground
    cinnamon
¼ cup water
4½ cups sliced, peeled
    peaches (about
    1½ pounds)
1 cup self-rising flour*
1 teaspoon sugar

¼ cup shortening
⅓ cup buttermilk or sour
    milk**
2 tablespoons butter,
    melted
2 tablespoons brown sugar
½ cup chopped pecans
Vanilla ice cream,
    half-and-half or light
    cream (optional)

**1** In a medium saucepan, combine the ¾ cup sugar, the cornstarch and cinnamon; stir in the water. Cook and stir till thickened and bubbly. Add peaches; return to boiling. Reduce heat and cook for 2 minutes more. Keep warm over very low heat.

**2** In a mixing bowl, combine the flour and the 1 teaspoon sugar. Using a pastry blender, cut in shortening till mixture resembles coarse crumbs. Add buttermilk and stir till just moistened. Turn out onto a lightly floured surface. Knead dough gently for 10 to 12 strokes. Roll into a 9×6-inch rectangle.

**3** Combine the butter and brown sugar. Spread over dough to within ½ inch of the edge. Sprinkle the pecans evenly over all. Roll up dough, jelly-roll style, starting with a short side. Cut the roll crosswise into six 1-inch-thick slices.

**4** Pour hot peach mixture into an ungreased 2-quart square (8×8×2-inch) baking dish. Place the pecan rolls on top. Bake in a 400° oven about 25 minutes or till golden brown. Cool on wire rack about 30 minutes. Serve cobbler warm. If you like, serve with ice cream or cream. Makes 6 servings.

**\*Note:** If you don't have self-rising flour in your pantry or can't find it at your supermarket, substitute a mixture of 1 cup *all-purpose flour*, 1 teaspoon *baking powder*, ½ teaspoon *salt* and ¼ teaspoon *baking soda*.

**\*\*Note:** To make sour milk, place 1 teaspoon *lemon juice* in a glass measuring cup. Pour in enough *milk* to make ⅓ cup liquid. Stir and let stand for 5 minutes.

## Can't-Miss Cobbler

An old-fashioned Midwestern specialty, cobbler provides a comforting conclusion to any meal. For company-perfect cobbler every time:

♦ Always use the size dish or baking pan specified in the recipe. Cobblers need room to bubble up during baking, so the dish must be deep enough to accommodate the bubbling. To avoid having the filling bubble over onto the floor of your oven, place a baking sheet underneath the baking dish or pan to catch spills.

♦ Make sure the filling is piping hot when you add the biscuit topper. Otherwise, the bottom of the topper won't cook all the way through.

♦ Check for doneness by inserting a wooden toothpick into the center of one or two of the biscuit mounds. The toothpick should come out clean. Be careful not to push the toothpick in the biscuits too far—you may coat it with the filling and not be able to tell if the topper is baked.

FAMILY-FAVORITE
PEACH-PECAN COBBLER

# PUNCH-BOWL CAKE

This splashy-looking dessert is a favorite at cookouts at Bill and Christine O'Neal's house in Bloomington, Illinois. What their guests don't know is that it's very easy to make. Use whatever type of berries that are in season.

1 package 1-layer-size yellow cake mix
1 8-ounce can pineapple chunks (juice-packed)
1 3-ounce package cream cheese, softened
1 4-serving-size instant vanilla pudding mix
2 ripe bananas, sliced

2 cups fresh strawberries, halved
½ cup fresh blueberries
1 8-ounce container frozen whipped dessert topping, thawed
⅓ cup chopped nuts
½ cup maraschino cherries
Chopped nuts (optional)

1 Prepare and bake cake mix in one 8-inch round layer according to package directions. Cool completely according to package directions. Split cake in half horizontally to make two layers.

2 Drain pineapple, reserving 2 tablespoons juice. Set pineapple aside. Beat reserved juice into cream cheese. Spread *half* of the cream cheese mixture over top of each cake layer. (Do not stack layers.) Set aside. Prepare pudding mix according to package directions.

3 In a 3-quart punch bowl or large glass salad bowl, place *half* of the pineapple chunks. Place one cake layer on top of pineapple, then arrange in layers *half* of the bananas, *half* of the strawberries, *half* of the blueberries and *half* of the prepared pudding. Spread with *half* of the whipped dessert topping. Sprinkle with *half* of the ⅓ cup nuts. Repeat layering, beginning with remaining pineapple and excluding the blueberries. Sprinkle with cherries and remaining blueberries. If you like, top with additional nuts. Makes 12 to 16 servings.

# GO-ANYWHERE RHUBARB SQUARES

This treat comes from retired Iowan Clarice Wellinghoff. When Clarice brought them to office gatherings, everyone loved these squares, which combine a rhubarb filling with a cookie crust.

1 cup all-purpose flour
⅓ cup sifted powdered sugar
⅓ cup butter
1 cup sugar

¼ cup all-purpose flour
2 slightly beaten eggs
1 teaspoon vanilla
3 cups finely chopped fresh or frozen rhubarb*

1 In a mixing bowl, combine the 1 cup flour and the powdered sugar. Using a pastry blender, cut in butter till mixture resembles coarse crumbs.

2 Pat the crumb mixture into the bottom of an ungreased 11×7×1½-inch or 9×9×2-inch baking pan. Bake in a 350° oven for 12 minutes.

3 In the mixing bowl, beat together sugar, the ¼ cup flour, the eggs and vanilla. Stir in rhubarb. Pour over warm crust in baking pan.

4 Return to oven and bake about 35 minutes more or till set. Serve warm, or cool in pan on wire rack. Store in the refrigerator. Makes 16 servings.

*Note: If using frozen rhubarb, thaw just enough so fruit chops easily.

# TAKE-ALONG BLACKBERRY SWIRL COBBLER

t family gatherings, Shirley Jo Card of Saranac, Michigan, treats everyone to her blackberry cobbler. The yummy blackberry filling is rolled up into flaky biscuits for a more special cobbler.

2 cups fresh or frozen
    blackberries
1 cup water
¾ cup sugar
¼ cup butter, melted
½ cup butter

1½ cups self-rising flour*
⅓ cup milk
½ teaspoon ground
    cinnamon
1 tablespoon sugar

1 If using frozen berries, thaw for 20 minutes; lightly mash any large berries.

2 For syrup, in a small saucepan, heat the water and ¾ cup sugar to boiling, stirring to dissolve sugar. Set aside. Pour the melted butter into a 10-inch pie plate or a 2-quart square (8×8×2-inch) baking dish. Set aside.

3 Using a pastry blender, cut the ½ cup butter into the flour till mixture resembles fine crumbs. Add the milk and stir till moistened.

4 Turn the dough out onto a lightly floured surface and knead 8 to 10 times. Roll out the dough to form a 10×8-inch rectangle. Sprinkle the rectangle with the berries and cinnamon.

5 Roll up, starting with one of the long sides. Cut crosswise into eight 1¼-inch-thick slices, tucking in any berries that fall out. Place, cut sides down, in the pie plate or baking dish. Pour syrup over the slices.

6 Place pie plate or baking dish on a baking sheet. Bake in a 350° oven for 45 minutes. Sprinkle with the 1 tablespoon sugar. Bake for 15 minutes more. Serve cobbler warm, or cool in pan on wire rack. Makes 8 servings.

**\*Note:** If you don't have self-rising flour in your pantry, substitute a mixture of 1½ cups *all-purpose flour*, 1½ teaspoons *baking powder*, ½ teaspoon *salt* and ¼ teaspoon *baking soda*.

**Carrying Hint:** Transport the fresh-from-the-oven cobbler in an insulated cooler to keep it warm.

---

# BAKED CARAMEL DELIGHT

his delicious, gooey dessert from The Patchwork Country Inn near Middlebury, Indiana, is as simple as the Amish lifestyle. But dessert doesn't have to be elaborate to be good. It will remind you of old-fashioned pudding cake.

½ cup butter
½ cup sugar
1½ cups all-purpose flour
1 teaspoon baking powder
⅛ teaspoon salt
½ cup milk

½ cup raisins
¾ cup packed brown sugar
1 cup cold water
    Whipped cream or ice
      cream

1 Grease an 8×8×2-inch baking pan. Set aside. In a mixing bowl, beat butter and sugar with an electric mixer till fluffy.

2 In a bowl, combine flour, baking powder and salt. Add the flour mixture and milk alternately to butter mixture, beating at low speed till just combined. Stir in the raisins.

3 Spread batter in the prepared pan. Sprinkle brown sugar over batter. Gradually pour the cold water over brown sugar.

4 Bake in a 350° oven about 40 minutes or till a wooden toothpick inserted in the center comes out clean. Serve warm with whipped cream or ice cream. Makes 8 servings.

# MINNESOTA WILD-RICE BREAD

In the Twin Cities, many Wuollet Bakery customers hollow out loaves of this Minnesota specialty and fill them with creamy onion dip to serve at parties. But it's so flavorful, the bread is also delicious all by itself.

¾ cup wild rice
2¼ cups water
1½ cups whole wheat flour
¾ cup rolled oats
½ cup dark rye flour
2 packages active dry yeast

1¼ cups warm water
  (120° to 130°)
⅓ cup honey
1½ teaspoons salt
2 to 2½ cups bread flour
Rolled oats (optional)
1 teaspoon cooking oil

1 Run *cold water* over the wild rice in a strainer for 1 minute, lifting rice to rinse thoroughly. In a saucepan, combine wild rice and the 2¼ cups water. Bring to boiling; reduce heat. Simmer, covered, 40 to 45 minutes or till just tender. Drain off any excess liquid. Fluff with a fork; cool till rice is just warm.

2 In a large mixing bowl, combine whole wheat flour, the ¾ cup oats, the rye flour and yeast. Stir in the 1¼ cups warm water, honey and salt. Stir in the wild rice. Cover; let stand at room temperature for 4 to 6 hours. (Or, refrigerate overnight.)

3 Using a wooden spoon, stir in as much of the bread flour as you can.

4 Turn out onto a lightly floured surface. Knead in enough of the remaining bread flour to make a moderately stiff dough that's smooth and elastic (6 to 8 minutes total). Shape into a ball. Place in a greased bowl; turn once. Cover; let rise in a warm place till doubled (1 to 1½ hours).

5 Punch dough down. Turn out onto a lightly floured surface. Divide in half. Cover; let rest for 10 minutes. Grease a large baking sheet. Shape each half of dough into a round loaf. Place on the prepared baking sheet; flatten slightly to 6 inches in diameter. (If you prefer a rounder loaf, flatten dough to 5 inches in diameter.) Cover; let rise till nearly doubled (40 to 50 minutes). If you like, sprinkle with additional oats.

6 Bake in a 375° oven for 40 to 45 minutes or till bread sounds hollow when tapped. If necessary, to prevent overbrowning, cover loosely with foil for the last 10 minutes of baking. Brush lightly with the oil. Transfer to wire racks; cool. Makes 2 loaves.

# QUICK RYE-BATTER BUNS

These buns are a tasty alternative to regular rye bread that's fish-boil fare in Wisconsin's Door County. Using fast-rising yeast helps dough rise in less time—about one-third less time—than regular yeast.

3 cups all-purpose flour
2 packages fast-rising
  active dry yeast
2 cups milk
½ cup packed dark brown
  sugar
3 tablespoons cooking oil

1½ teaspoons salt
2 eggs
1 teaspoon caraway seed
  (optional)
2 cups rye flour
Milk
Caraway seed (optional)

1 In a large bowl, combine the all-purpose flour and yeast. In saucepan, heat the 2 cups milk, brown sugar, oil and salt till warm (120° to 130°), stirring constantly. Add to flour mixture. Add eggs and, if you like, 1 teaspoon caraway seed.

2 Beat with electric mixer on low speed for 30 seconds, scraping sides of bowl. Beat on high speed for 3 minutes. Return to low speed and beat in the rye flour. Grease twenty-four 2½-inch muffin cups. Fill prepared muffin cups ½ full with batter. Cover and let the dough rise till doubled (about 25 minutes).

3 Bake buns in a 400° oven for 10 minutes. Brush the buns with milk. If you like, sprinkle the tops with additional caraway seed. Bake for 5 to 10 minutes more or till done. Remove the buns from the pans; cool on wire racks. Makes 24 buns.

MINNESOTA
WILD-RICE BREAD

# HEARTY WHOLE-GRAIN BREAD

racked wheat adds crunch to the crust of this easy version of a bread made at the Wuollet Bakery in Minneapolis. The bakery makes its whole-grain loaves the Scandinavian way—with rye flour.

| | |
|---|---|
| ½ cup cracked-wheat cereal | 1½ cups warm water |
| 2½ to 3 cups bread flour | (120° to 130°) |
| 2 packages active dry yeast | 1¾ cups dark rye flour |
| 2 teaspoons salt | 1 beaten egg yolk |
| | 1 tablespoon water |

**1** In a bowl, pour enough *boiling water* over the cracked-wheat cereal to cover; let stand for 5 minutes. Drain well.

**2** In a large bowl, stir together *1 cup* of the bread flour, the yeast and salt. Add the warm water. Beat with an electric mixer on low speed for 30 seconds, scraping sides of bowl. Beat on high for 3 minutes. Using a spoon, stir in the cracked-wheat cereal, rye flour, and as much of the remaining bread flour as you can.

**3** Turn out onto lightly floured surface. Knead in enough of the remaining bread flour to make a moderately stiff dough that's smooth and elastic (6 to 8 minutes total). Shape into a ball. Place in greased bowl; turn once. Cover and let rise in a warm place till doubled (about 1 hour).

**4** Punch dough down. Turn dough out onto a lightly floured surface. Divide in half. Cover; let rest for 10 minutes. Grease a large baking sheet. Shape each half of dough into a round loaf. Place on the prepared baking sheet; flatten slightly to 5 inches in diameter. With a very sharp knife, make 3 or 4 slashes ¼ inch deep across top of each loaf. Cover; let rise till nearly doubled (30 to 45 minutes).

**5** Brush tops of loaves with a mixture of the egg yolk and the 1 tablespoon water.

**6** Bake in a 375° oven about 40 minutes or till bread sounds hollow when tapped. If necessary to prevent overbrowning, cover loosely with foil for the last 10 to 20 minutes of baking. Transfer to wire racks; cool. Makes 2 loaves.

# DORIE'S ZWIEBACH

hen Dorie and Linden Theissen opened Olde Towne Restaurant in Hillsboro, Kansas, they featured specialties such as zwiebach. It isn't the crisp cracker variety, however. Theirs is a buttery, two-story roll.

| | |
|---|---|
| ½ cup potato water or water | 1 teaspoon salt |
| ¼ cup sugar | 5¼ to 5¾ cups all-purpose |
| 1 package active dry yeast | flour |
| 1 cup milk | 1 slightly beaten egg |
| ¾ cup butter | Nonstick spray coating |

**1** In a bowl, stir together the water, sugar and yeast. Let stand till yeast dissolves. In a saucepan, heat the milk, butter and salt till just warm (120° to 130°).

**2** In a mixing bowl, combine butter mixture with *2 cups* of the flour. Add egg and the yeast mixture.

**3** Beat with an electric mixer for 30 seconds, scraping sides of bowl. Beat on high speed for 3 minutes. Using a spoon, stir in as much of the remaining flour as you can.

**4** Turn out onto a floured surface. Knead in enough of the remaining flour to make a moderately soft dough that's smooth and elastic (3 to 5 minutes total). Shape into a ball. Place in a greased bowl; turn once. Cover; let rise in a warm place till doubled (about 1 hour). Punch dough down. Turn out onto a lightly floured surface. Cover and let rest for 10 minutes.

**5** Spray a large baking sheet with nonstick coating. For each zwiebach, pinch off enough dough to make a 1½-inch ball. Place the dough balls on the prepared baking sheet. Top each dough ball with a 1-inch ball of dough. Press a lightly floured finger into center of the balls.

**6** Bake in a 350° oven for 15 to 20 minutes. Transfer to wire racks; cool slightly. Serve warm. Makes 20 rolls.

# Kansas Honey-Wheat-Sunflower Bread

Try a thick, warm slice of this official Kansas bread (given the honors by the state's legislature). Studded with sunflower nuts and sweetened with honey, the flavorful bread is like eating honey cake.

2 cups lukewarm water
   (120° to 130°)
2¾ to 3¼ cups bread flour
   or all-purpose flour
2 packages active dry yeast
1 tablespoon sugar
2 cups whole wheat flour
1 cup rolled oats

⅓ cup nonfat dry milk
   powder
¼ cup butter, softened
¼ cup honey
2 teaspoons salt
1 cup unsalted sunflower
   nuts

1 In a large mixing bowl, combine the water, *2 cups* of the bread flour or all-purpose flour, the yeast and sugar. Beat with electric mixer on low speed for 3 minutes, scraping sides of bowl. Cover; let rise till doubled (about 30 minutes). The mixture will become spongy.

2 Stir in whole wheat flour, oats, milk powder, butter, honey and salt. Mix well. Stir in sunflower nuts. Using a wooden spoon, stir in as much of the remaining bread or all-purpose flour as you can.

3 Turn out onto a floured surface; knead in enough of the remaining flour to make a moderately stiff dough that's smooth and elastic (6 to 8 minutes total). Place the dough in a greased bowl; turn. Cover; let rise in a warm place till doubled (30 to 45 minutes).

4 Punch the dough down. Turn the dough out onto a lightly floured surface. Divide the dough in half. Cover; let rest for 10 minutes. Grease two 8×4×2-inch loaf pans.

5 Shape each half of dough into a loaf. Place in prepared pans. Cover; let rise in warm place till almost doubled (about 30 minutes).

6 Bake loaves in a 375° oven about 35 minutes or till bread sounds hollow when tapped. If necessary to prevent overbrowning, cover loosely with foil for the last 15 minutes of baking. Remove loaves from pans. Cool on wire racks. Makes 2 loaves.

# Sunny Corn Muffins

The bakery crew at Amish Acres in Nappanee, Indiana, makes cookies, cakes, pies, yeast breads and muffins to serve in the dining room and sell in the restaurant's shop. These corn muffins are best-sellers.

1 cup all-purpose flour
1 cup cornmeal
¼ cup packed brown sugar
2 teaspoons cream of tartar
½ teaspoon baking soda

¼ teaspoon salt
1 beaten egg
1 cup milk
¼ cup butter, melted

1 Grease twelve 2½-inch muffin cups. Set aside. In a medium mixing bowl, combine flour, cornmeal, brown sugar, cream of tartar, baking soda and salt.

2 In a bowl, combine egg, milk and melted butter. Add all at once to the flour mixture. Stir till just moistened. Fill prepared muffin cups ⅔ full with batter.

3 Bake in a 400° oven about 20 minutes or till lightly browned. Serve warm. Makes 12 muffins.

# FRUITY STREUSEL-TOPPED COFFEE CAKE

lever cooks in Syracuse, Nebraska, streamlined this old-fashioned favorite by starting with frozen bread dough. The coffee cake disappears fast at the town's Octoberfest. Vary the fruit according to your whim.

1 16-ounce loaf frozen
    white bread dough,
    thawed
1 beaten egg
½ cup sugar
¼ cup half-and-half or light
    cream
4 cups thinly sliced peeled
    apples, raspberries,
    sliced strawberries
    and/or blueberries

1 cup all-purpose flour
½ cup sugar
½ teaspoon ground
    cinnamon
½ cup butter
    Fresh apple slices,
    raspberries,
    strawberries
    and/or blueberries
    (optional)

**1** Grease a 15×10×1-inch baking pan. On a lightly floured surface, roll dough into a 17×12-inch rectangle.* Fit dough into the bottom and up the sides of the prepared pan. Cover; let rise in a warm place till nearly doubled (30 to 40 minutes).

**2** In a small bowl, stir together egg, ½ cup sugar and the half-and-half or cream. Arrange the 4 cups fruit on dough in pan. Spoon egg mixture over fruit.

**3** In a medium mixing bowl, stir together flour, ½ cup sugar and the cinnamon. Using a pastry blender, cut in butter till mixture resembles coarse crumbs. Sprinkle over fruit.

**4** Bake cake in a 375° oven about 25 minutes or till the edges are lightly browned. Serve cake warm. If you like, garnish each serving with fresh fruit. Makes 12 servings.

**\*Note:** Rolling out the thawed bread dough may take a while, because the dough can be very elastic. One technique is to roll out the dough as far as possible, cover with plastic wrap and wait about 5 minutes, then roll again. Repeat till of desired dimension.

---

# SOUR CREAM SWIRL COFFEE CAKE

 layer of brown sugar, cinnamon and pecans swirls through the center of this coffee cake from the Lantz House Inn in Centerville, Indiana. Include it as part of a brunch menu or cut slices for afternoon coffee or tea.

2 cups sugar
1 cup butter, melted
2 eggs
1 cup dairy sour cream
½ teaspoon vanilla
2 cups all-purpose flour
1 teaspoon baking powder

¼ teaspoon salt
⅔ cup chopped pecans
2 tablespoons brown sugar
1½ teaspoons ground
    cinnamon
    Sifted powdered sugar

**1** Grease and flour a 10-inch tube pan or a 10-inch fluted tube pan. Set aside. In a large mixing bowl, beat sugar and butter with electric mixer till mixture is thoroughly combined. Add eggs; beat well. Beat in sour cream and vanilla till just combined.

**2** In a small bowl, mix the 2 cups flour, baking powder and salt. Beat into creamed mixture till combined. Pour *half* of the batter into prepared pan.

**3** Stir together pecans, brown sugar and cinnamon. Sprinkle *half* of the mixture on top of batter in pan. Carefully spread remaining batter on top of nut mixture. Sprinkle with remaining nut mixture; press lightly into batter.

**4** Bake in a 350° oven for 45 to 50 minutes or till a wooden toothpick inserted near the center comes out clean. Remove cake from oven; cool for 5 minutes. Invert cake onto a serving plate. Dust with powdered sugar. Serve warm or cool. Makes 12 to 16 servings.

**JAM-FILLED TEA COOKIES**
(back plate, see recipe, page 58)
**FRUITY STREUSEL-TOPPED
COFFEE CAKE** (front plate, see
recipe, page 42)

# RED RIVER CEREAL MUFFINS

hen Canadian Maple Leaf Foods Co. began exporting cracked-wheat Red River cereal to the United States, the Wuollet Bakery in Minneapolis added it to these muffins. Brown sugar and honey sweeten these morsels.

2 cups water
⅓ cup shortening or cooking oil
1 cup Red River Cereal or cracked-wheat cereal (6 ounces)
2½ cups bread flour
½ cup nonfat dry milk powder
2½ teaspoons baking powder
1 teaspoon ground nutmeg
¼ teaspoon salt
3 eggs
¾ cup packed brown sugar
¾ cup raisins
1 tablespoon honey

1 Grease twenty-four 2½-inch muffin cups or line with paper bake cups. In a small saucepan, bring water and shortening or oil to boiling. Stir in cereal. Cook and stir for 1 minute. Remove from heat; let stand to cool to room temperature.

2 In a large mixing bowl, combine the flour, milk powder, baking powder, nutmeg and salt. Make a well in the center.

3 In another bowl, beat eggs. Stir in brown sugar, raisins and honey. Stir in cereal mixture. Add all at once to flour mixture. Stir till just moistened (the batter should be lumpy and thick). Fill prepared muffin pans ¾ full with batter.*

4 Bake in a 400° oven for 20 to 25 minutes or till golden brown. Remove from pans. Serve warm. Makes 24 muffins.

*Note: Since these muffins don't rise as much as some, fill the muffin pans ¾ full with batter.

## Muffin-Making Reminders

Whether served warm from the oven for breakfast, with soup come lunchtime or as the perfect accompaniment to a tossed salad at dinner, muffins are a Midwestern favorite. Here are some baking suggestions from Heartland cooks:

♦ For nicely rounded muffins with no ledges around the rims, grease the sides of muffin cups just halfway up.

♦ Once you add the liquid to the dry ingredients, stir the ingredients only till they are just moistened. The batter should still be lumpy. If you overmix, the muffins will be tough and may have peaks and tunnels.

♦ Once you have the batter in the muffin cups, bake the muffins immediately to retain the optimal leavening power of the baking powder or baking soda.

♦ Watch the muffins closely as they bake so they don't overbake. They're done when the tops turn a golden brown.

# PRIZE-WINNING
## PLEASURES

Cooks who earn a special ribbon or recognition for their baking efforts pride themselves on their winnings. You'll win, too, when you bake from this cream-of-the-crop collection selected from contests across the Heartland.

*Numbers in italic type indicate a photograph.*

# SNAPPY GINGERSNAP COOKIES

rizewinner Philip Maschka, who summers at Iowa's West Lake Okoboji, bakes these classics to submit at the Clay County Fair. His wife, Ruthann, provides the recipe. Philip recommends sampling them warm.

¾ cup shortening
1 cup packed brown sugar
1½ teaspoons baking soda
1 teaspoon ground ginger
1 teaspoon ground cinnamon
½ teaspoon salt
½ teaspoon ground cloves
¼ cup molasses
1 egg
2¼ cups all-purpose flour
Sugar

**1** In a large mixing bowl, beat the shortening with electric mixer for 30 seconds.

**2** Add the brown sugar, baking soda, ginger, cinnamon, salt and cloves; beat till thoroughly combined. Beat in the molasses and egg.

**3** Beat in as much of the flour as you can with the mixer. Stir in any remaining flour with a spoon.

**4** Cover and refrigerate the dough for 2 hours or till it's easy to handle.

**5** Shape dough into 1-inch balls; roll in sugar. Place 2 inches apart on ungreased cookie sheets.

**6** Bake in a 375° oven for 8 to 9 minutes or till set and tops are cracked. (Don't bake on lower oven rack and don't overbake.) Cool cookies on waxed paper or a wire rack. (Cookies will be softer if cooled on waxed paper.) Makes about 60 cookies.

# RASPBERRY SODA-CRACKER PIE

eba DeBlieck of Chaska, Minnesota, proved her talents at a Raspberry Festival baking contest in Hopkins, Minnesota. Taking first place, the meringue-crust pie is based on a recipe from her late mother-in-law, Grace.

4 egg whites
¼ teaspoon cream of tartar
1 teaspoon vanilla
1 cup sugar
16 saltine crackers, crushed
½ cup chopped pecans
1 8-ounce carton whipping cream
⅓ cup sugar
1 teaspoon vanilla
2 to 3 cups fresh or frozen raspberries, blueberries, sliced strawberries or blackberries

**1** Grease and flour a 9-inch pie plate. Set aside. In a large mixing bowl, beat egg whites and cream of tartar with an electric mixer on medium speed till foamy. Beat in 1 teaspoon vanilla. Gradually beat in the 1 cup sugar till stiff peaks form (tips stand straight). Fold in crackers and pecans.

**2** Transfer the egg white mixture to prepared pie plate, spreading over bottom and sides. Bake in a 325° oven for 35 to 40 minutes or till golden brown. Cool on a wire rack.

**3** For filling, in a mixing bowl, beat cream, the ⅓ cup sugar and 1 teaspoon vanilla till soft peaks form. Fold in berries. Spoon into crust. Store in the refrigerator. Makes 8 servings.

# WHOLE WHEAT-OATMEAL-RAISIN BREAD

"ince I have the time and energy, I try to do things the old-fashioned way," says Iowa baker Philip Maschka. "I don't use mixers, microwaves or bread machines." However, *you* can use your mixer for ease in making.

2 cups boiling water
1 cup rolled oats
½ cup honey
2 tablespoons butter
1½ teaspoons salt
2 packages active dry yeast
½ cup warm water
   (105° to 115°)

2 cups whole wheat flour
4 to 4½ cups bread flour
   Nonstick spray coating
1 teaspoon ground
   cinnamon
1 cup raisins
   Ground cinnamon

1 In a large bowl, combine the 2 cups boiling water, the oats, honey, butter and salt. Set aside to cool.

2 In a small bowl, soften yeast in the ½ cup warm water, stirring with a spoon to mix. Let stand for 10 to 15 minutes.

3 When the oatmeal mixture has cooled to lukewarm, stir in the yeast mixture. Add the whole wheat flour and beat till smooth.

4 Add the bread flour, *1 cup* at a time, mixing thoroughly. When the dough becomes too thick to mix with a spoon, knead by hand on a lightly floured surface. Knead in enough of the remaining flour to make a moderately stiff dough that's smooth and elastic (6 to 8 minutes total).

5 Spray a large bowl with nonstick coating. Shape dough into a ball. Place in the prepared bowl. Spray top of dough with nonstick coating. Cover with waxed paper and let dough rise in a warm place till doubled in size (about 1 hour).

6 Punch dough down. Turn out onto a lightly floured surface. Divide dough in half. Cover and let rest for 10 minutes.

7 Grease two 8×4×2-inch loaf pans. Set aside. Roll half of dough to a rectangle about 12×9 inches. Sprinkle generously with *half* of the 1 teaspoon cinnamon and *half* of the raisins. Roll up from a short side. Pinch edges and ends to seal. Place in one of the prepared pans. Repeat with the remaining dough, remaining cinnamon and remaining raisins.

8 Cover dough with waxed paper and let rise in a warm place till about ½ inch above the edge of the pan (25 to 30 minutes). Spray the loaves with nonstick coating; sprinkle with additional cinnamon.

9 Bake in a 350° oven for 35 to 40 minutes or till loaves sound hollow when tapped. If necessary to prevent overbrowning, cover loosely with foil for the last 10 minutes of baking. Remove loaves from pans. Cool on wire racks. Makes 2 loaves.

## Save Time with Fast-Rise Yeast

Using fast-rising yeast can be a timesaving shortcut for bread bakers. It can cut the dough's rising time by a third. The yeast bread and roll recipes in this book were tested with regular active dry yeast. However, you can prepare these recipes (except for any yeast doughs requiring a refrigerated rise) using the fast-rising active dry yeast. Follow the same directions, but check rising earlier.

# QUICK-AND-EASY PUMPKIN PIE BARS

These spicy pumpkin bars start with a yellow cake mix. Ryann, Leslie and Rachel Chilton won first place with this treat in the children's bars category at the Harvest Baking contest in New Albany, Indiana.

1 package 2-layer-size
   yellow cake mix
½ cup butter, melted and
   cooled
3 eggs
1 16-ounce can pumpkin
1 5-ounce can (⅔ cup)
   evaporated milk
½ cup packed brown sugar
2½ teaspoons pumpkin pie
   spice

2 tablespoons sugar
2 tablespoons butter,
   softened
1 teaspoon ground
   cinnamon or pumpkin
   pie spice
Whipped cream
Pumpkin pie spice
   (optional)

1 Combine the dry cake mix, melted butter and *one* of the eggs; beat till combined. Set aside *1 cup* of the cake-mix mixture.

2 Spread the remaining cake-mix mixture in an ungreased 13×9×2-inch baking pan, pressing to form an even crust.

3 In a medium mixing bowl, beat together the remaining eggs, the pumpkin, evaporated milk, brown sugar and the 2½ teaspoons pumpkin pie spice. Pour the pumpkin mixture over crust in prepared pan.

4 Combine the reserved cake-mix mixture, the sugar, the 2 tablespoons softened butter and the cinnamon. Dot evenly over the pumpkin mixture. Bake in a 350° oven for 45 to 50 minutes or till a wooden toothpick inserted near the center comes out clean.

5 Cool in pan on wire rack. Cut into 32 triangles. Serve with whipped cream. If you like, sprinkle whipped cream with additional pumpkin pie spice. Makes 12 servings.

# MAXINE'S BLACK WALNUT QUICK BREAD

For Indiana's Elkhart Country Fair, Maxine Nelson makes this winning quick bread with sour cream and a big cup of black walnuts. If you don't have the more distinctive-flavored black walnuts, use regular walnuts.

1 cup sugar
1 8-ounce carton dairy sour
   cream
1 egg
1 teaspoon vanilla
1¾ cups all-purpose flour

1 teaspoon baking powder
½ teaspoon baking soda
¼ teaspoon salt
1 cup chopped black
   walnuts

1 Grease and flour an 8×4×2-inch loaf pan. Set aside. In a mixing bowl, beat sugar, sour cream, egg and vanilla till thoroughly combined.

2 Stir together the flour, baking powder, baking soda and salt. Stir into sour cream mixture. Fold in the walnuts. Pour into prepared pan.

3 Bake in a 325° oven about 65 minutes or till a wooden toothpick inserted near the center comes out clean. Cool on a wire rack for 10 minutes. Remove from pan; cool on rack. Makes 1 loaf.

# BROWNIE BOMBS

**O**ne of the contestants in *Midwest Living*® magazine's Chocolate Champs contest, Cheryl Setty of West Carrollton, Ohio, tops her winning dessert with a cheesecake layer. Then she adds more chocolate batter.

| | |
|---|---|
| 4 ounces unsweetened chocolate | ⅓ cup sugar |
| ½ cup butter | 4 teaspoons all-purpose flour |
| 1⅓ cups sugar | 1 egg |
| ½ teaspoon vanilla | ¼ teaspoon vanilla |
| 3 eggs | Nonstick spray coating |
| ¾ cup all-purpose flour | ½ cup semisweet chocolate pieces |
| 1 8-ounce package cream cheese, softened | |

**1** In a heavy medium saucepan, melt unsweetened chocolate and butter over low heat. Remove from heat. Stir in the 1⅓ cups sugar and the ½ teaspoon vanilla. Cool for 15 minutes. Beat in the 3 eggs and the ¾ cup flour.

**2** In a medium mixing bowl, stir together cream cheese, the ⅓ cup sugar, the 4 teaspoons flour, the 1 egg and the ¼ teaspoon vanilla.

**3** Spray an 8×8×2-inch baking pan with nonstick spray coating. Spread ⅔ *of chocolate batter* into pan. Spoon cheese mixture over batter. Dollop with the remaining chocolate batter.

**4** Bake in a 350° oven for 20 minutes. Sprinkle with chocolate pieces. Bake for 12 minutes more. Cool in pan on wire rack. Cover; store in refrigerator. Before serving, let stand at room temperature for 30 minutes. Cut into squares. Makes 16 servings.

---

# NUTTY CARROT BREAD

**A** sweet-tart lemon glaze tops this moist quick bread. It won Maxine Nelson of Elkhart, Indiana, a blue ribbon at the Elkhart County Fair. The Lemon Glaze makes it a little more special than other quick breads.

| | |
|---|---|
| ¾ cup sugar | ½ teaspoon salt |
| ¾ cup cooking oil | 1½ cups finely shredded carrots |
| 2 eggs | 1½ cups chopped walnuts |
| 1 teaspoon vanilla | Lemon Glaze (recipe follows) |
| 1½ cups all-purpose flour | Shredded lemon peel (optional) |
| 1½ teaspoons ground cinnamon | |
| 1 teaspoon baking soda | |

**1** Grease and flour a 9×5×3-inch or an 8×4×2-inch loaf pan. In a large mixing bowl, beat together sugar, oil, eggs and vanilla.

**2** In a medium mixing bowl, stir together the flour, cinnamon, baking soda and salt. Stir into the egg mixture till thoroughly combined.

**3** Stir in carrots and walnuts till thoroughly combined. Pour into prepared pan.

**4** Bake in a 350° oven for 1 hour or till a wooden toothpick inserted in the center comes out clean. Cool on wire rack for 10 minutes. Remove from pan and cool completely on wire rack.

**5** Drizzle Lemon Glaze over cooled bread. If you like, sprinkle with lemon peel. Makes 1 loaf.

**Lemon Glaze:** In a small mixing bowl, stir together ½ cup *powdered sugar*, 1 teaspoon finely shredded *lemon peel* and 1 tablespoon *lemon juice* till smooth.

# CARROT-ZUCCHINI CAKE

 A pecan-cream cheese icing tops this impressive carrot-zucchini cake that won Maxine Nelson of Elkhart, Indiana, a red ribbon. Try this baker's masterpiece in a rectangular pan or as a layer cake.

2½ cups all-purpose flour
2 teaspoons baking powder
1¾ teaspoons ground cinnamon
½ teaspoon baking soda
½ teaspoon salt
½ teaspoon ground nutmeg
1 cup butter
1¾ cups sugar
1 teaspoon vanilla

4 eggs
½ cup evaporated milk
1½ teaspoons lemon juice
1½ cups finely shredded carrots
1½ cups finely shredded unpeeled zucchini
¾ cup finely chopped pecans
Pecan-Cream Cheese Icing (recipe follows)

**1** Grease and flour a 13×9×2-inch baking pan. (Or, grease and flour two 9×1½-inch round baking pans.) Set aside.

**2** In a mixing bowl, stir together flour, baking powder, cinnamon, baking soda, salt and nutmeg.

**3** In a large mixing bowl, beat butter with an electric mixer about 30 seconds or till softened. Add sugar and vanilla; beat till thoroughly combined. Add eggs, one at a time, beating well after each addition.

**4** Stir together the evaporated milk and lemon juice. Add the flour mixture and milk mixture alternately to egg mixture, beating on low speed after each addition till just combined.

**5** Stir in the carrots and zucchini; fold in pecans. Pour batter into the prepared pan(s).

**6** Bake in a 350° oven for 45 to 50 minutes for the 13×9-inch pan (or about 40 minutes for 9-inch pans) or till a wooden toothpick inserted near the center(s) comes out clean. Thoroughly cool 13×9-inch cake in pan on a wire rack. (Or, for round layers, cool in pans on wire racks for 10 minutes. Remove cakes from pans. Cool completely on wire racks.)

**7** Frost the top of cake in 13×9-inch pan with the Pecan-Cream Cheese Icing. (Or, fill and frost 9-inch layers with icing.) Makes 12 servings.

**Pecan-Cream Cheese Icing:** Combine two 3-ounce packages *cream cheese*, softened; 4 teaspoons *milk* and 2 teaspoons *vanilla*. Beat with electric mixer till smooth and fluffy. Gradually add 4½ cups sifted *powdered sugar* to the creamed mixture; beat till smooth and fluffy. Stir in ½ cup finely chopped *pecans*. If necessary, add additional *milk* to make of spreading consistency.

## Softening Savvy

Are you ready to use your cream cheese, but it's still brick hard? Speed up softening by cutting it into 1-inch cubes and letting it stand at room temperature for 1 hour. Or, if you're really in a hurry, soften the cream cheese in your microwave oven. Unwrap the cream cheese and place it in a microwave-safe bowl. Heat 3 ounces on 100% power (high) for 15 to 30 seconds or 8 ounces for 30 to 60 seconds.

# COOKIES-AND-CREAM CAKE

Cake mix and sandwich cookies are combined in this easy-on the-cook dessert that earned Pat Habiger of Spearville, Kansas, a winning spot in *Midwest Living®* magazine's Chocolate Champs contest.

1 package 2-layer-size
    white cake mix
1¼ cups water
⅓ cup cooking oil
3 egg whites
1 cup coarsely crushed
    chocolate sandwich
    cookies with white
    filling

Creamy White Frosting
    (recipe follows)
2 ounces semisweet
    chocolate
1 teaspoon shortening
Broken chocolate
    sandwich cookies with
    white filling (optional)

**1** Grease and flour two 9×1½-inch round baking pans. Prepare the cake mix according to package directions, except using the water, oil and egg whites. Fold in the crushed sandwich cookies. Spread batter into prepared pans.

**2** Bake in a 350° oven for 25 to 30 minutes or till a wooden toothpick inserted in centers comes out clean. Cool on wire racks for 10 minutes. Remove layers from pans and cool completely on wire racks.

**3** Fill and frost the cake layers with Creamy White Frosting. In a heavy small saucepan, melt the semisweet chocolate and shortening over very low heat. Drizzle mixture over the top of cake. If you like, decorate cake with additional broken sandwich cookies. Makes 16 servings.

**Creamy White Frosting:** In a large mixing bowl, beat 1 cup *shortening* and 1 tablespoon *vanilla* with an electric mixer for 30 seconds. Slowly add 2½ cups sifted *powdered sugar*, beating mixture well. Add 2 tablespoons *milk*. Slowly beat in 2 cups more sifted *powdered sugar* and 2 to 3 tablespoons more *milk* till frosting is of spreading consistency.

---

# BLUE RIBBON ANGEL FOOD CAKE

Julie Herron of Salem, Ohio, won a blue ribbon at Ohio's Canfield Fair with her mother's angel food cake recipe. For a dessert that's special enough for company, serve mixed fresh fruit or a fruit sauce over the cake.

12 egg whites (1½ cups)
1½ cups sifted powdered
    sugar
1 cup sifted cake flour
1½ teaspoons cream of tartar

¼ teaspoon salt
1 cup sugar
1½ teaspoons vanilla
½ teaspoon almond extract

**1** Allow egg whites to stand at room temperature for 30 minutes. Sift together powdered sugar and cake flour; set aside.

**2** In a large mixing bowl, beat egg whites, cream of tartar and salt till foamy. Gradually add sugar, *2 tablespoons* at a time, beating on high speed till stiff peaks form (tips stand straight). Quickly beat in vanilla and almond extract. Sprinkle flour-sugar mixture, *¼ cup* at a time, over beaten egg whites, folding gently just till flour-sugar mixture disappears.

**3** Spoon batter into an ungreased 10-inch tube pan. Gently cut through batter with a knife or spatula to remove large air pockets.

**4** Bake in a 375° oven for 35 to 40 minutes or till top springs back when touched lightly with your finger. Invert cake in pan on a funnel; let the cake cool completely. Loosen the sides of the cake with a narrow-bladed spatula or knife. Remove cake from pan. Makes 12 servings.

# SPECIAL–DAY DELIGHTS

**N**otable occasions warrant baking something out-of-the ordinary. Choose one of these baked favorites—from cookies to cheesecakes—for your next important day.

## Bars and Cookies
Candy-Cane Swirl Cookies **59**
Cinnamon-Cardamom Crisps **59**
Decadent Chocolate-Filled Bars **62**
Delicate Lemon Snowdrops **63**
Dutch Almond Bars **60**, *61*
Fancy Raspberry Ribbons **62**
Jam-Filled Tea Cookies *43*, **58**
Norwegian Fina-Grubber **63**
Swedish Spritz Cookies **60**, *61*

## Breads, Rolls, Buns, Scones, Muffins
Almond-Kissed Hot-Cross Buns **84**, *85*
Bay View Inn's Herb Rolls **88**
Breakfast Puffs **92**
Cinnamon Swirl Bread **86**
Honey-Rhubarb Muffins **92**, *93*
Lemony Tea Bread **91**
Mandel Bread **84**
Maple-Pecan Scones **91**
Never-Fail Cinnamon Rolls **88**, *89*

## Cakes
Angie's Pumpkin Roll **74**
Cherry-Vanilla Spiral Cake **70**
Dark Chocolate-Nut Cake **71**
Lemon Cream Dessert Cake **72**, *73*
Orange-Slice Gumdrop Cake **74**
Tapawingo's Pear and Ginger Cake **75**

## Cheesecakes
Amaretto Cheesecake **80**
Cheery Mint-Chocolate Cheesecake **76**, *77*
Decadent Hazelnut Cheesecake **80**
Joanne's German Chocolate Cheesecake **78**, *79*
White Chocolate Cheesecake **76**

## Coffee Cake
Applesauce-Date Coffee Cake **90**

## Pies and Tarts
Best Peach Pie **64**, *65*
Chocolate-Raspberry Fudge Tart **68**
Clifton Mill Chocolate-Pecan Pie **66**
Cranberry-Raspberry Pie **66**
Double-Crust Pastry **64**
Reunion Sweet Potato Pie **67**
Summertime Choose-A-Fruit Tart **68**, *69*

## Miscellaneous
Black Forest Cream Puffs **81**
Caramel Apple-Walnut Squares **83**
Gingerbread Pudding with Brandy Cream Sauce **83**
Norwegian-Style Sour Cream Twists **86**
Steamed Cranberry Pudding with Hard Sauce **82**
Swedish Pear Tosa **82**
Triple Chocolate Biscotti **58**

*Numbers in italic type indicate a photograph.*

# TRIPLE CHOCOLATE BISCOTTI

t the Wuollet Bakery in Minnesota's Twin Cities, longtime employee Sue Teleen created this popular treat. Drizzle slices of the crunchy, mocha-flavored biscotti with melted white chocolate for a decorative finish.

3¼ cups all-purpose flour
1¾ cups finely chopped
    hazelnuts (filberts)
⅔ cup miniature semisweet
    chocolate pieces
½ cup unsweetened cocoa
    powder
2 tablespoons instant
    espresso powder

1½ teaspoons baking powder
1 teaspoon salt
½ teaspoon baking soda
½ cup butter
2 cups sugar
3 eggs
3 ounces white chocolate or
    white baking bar
1 tablespoon shortening

**1** In a large mixing bowl, stir together flour, hazelnuts, chocolate pieces, cocoa powder, espresso powder, baking powder, salt and baking soda.

**2** In a very large mixing bowl, beat butter with an electric mixer about 30 seconds or till softened. Gradually add sugar. Add eggs, one at a time, beating after each addition. Stir in the flour mixture.

**3** Divide dough in half. Shape each portion into a 12×2-inch log. Place logs 4 inches apart on ungreased cookie sheet. Bake in a 375° oven for 25 to 30 minutes or till lightly browned and edges are firm. Cool on cookie sheet for 1 hour.

**4** Cut each log diagonally into ½-inch-thick slices. Lay slices, cut sides down, on the ungreased cookie sheet. Bake in a 325° oven for 5 minutes; turn pieces over. Bake 5 to 10 minutes more or till dry and crisp. Remove cookies to wire racks; cool.

**5** In a heavy small saucepan, melt white chocolate or baking bar and shortening over low heat, stirring occasionally. Drizzle over slices. Makes about 40 cookies.

# JAM-FILLED TEA COOKIES

ine bread crumbs top these crisp fruit-filled cookies (also known as *spitzbuben*). They're one of the cookie specialties you'll find at the Octoberfest in Hays, Kansas. (Pictured on page 43.)

1 cup butter
½ cup sugar
½ teaspoon vanilla
2 cups all-purpose flour
1 egg yolk

1 teaspoon milk
Fine dry bread crumbs
Jam
Powdered sugar (optional)

**1** In a large mixing bowl, beat butter with an electric mixer about 30 seconds or till softened. Beat in sugar and vanilla. Add flour; beat till combined. Divide dough in half. Cover; refrigerate 2 to 24 hours.

**2** On a lightly floured surface, roll each portion of dough to ¼-inch thickness. Cut with a 2½- to 3-inch diamond-shaped cutter, or use a knife or pastry wheel to cut into diamonds.

**3** Place cookies on an ungreased cookie sheet. In a small bowl, mix egg yolk and milk. Brush onto tops of cookies; sprinkle lightly with bread crumbs.

**4** Bake in 375° oven about 10 minutes or till edges are lightly browned. Remove cookies to wire racks; cool.

**5** Spread jam on the flat sides of *half* of the cookies. Top with the remaining cookies, flat sides down. If you like, sift powdered sugar over cookies. Makes about 24 cookies.

# CINNAMON-CARDAMOM CRISPS

inda Shuster of Chagrin Falls, Ohio, shares her favorite recipe (also called *mandel kager*). These crunchy, spiced cookies are glazed with egg and topped with sliced almonds. Cardamom adds a spicy-sweet flavor.

1⅔ cups all-purpose flour
2 teaspoons ground cinnamon
1½ teaspoons ground cardamom
½ teaspoon baking powder
1 cup butter, softened
½ cup sugar
1 egg
½ cup ground almonds
1 slightly beaten egg yolk
1 tablespoon water
Sliced almonds

1 In a medium mixing bowl, stir together the flour, cinnamon, cardamom and baking powder.

2 In a large bowl, beat butter, sugar and the whole egg with an electric mixer till thoroughly combined. Add flour mixture and ground almonds; beat well. Cover; refrigerate about 2 hours or till easy to handle.

3 Shape dough into ¾-inch balls. Place on ungreased cookie sheets about 2 inches apart. Flatten the balls slightly. Combine egg yolk and water. Brush the tops with egg yolk mixture; sprinkle with sliced almonds.

4 Bake in a 375° oven for 10 to 12 minutes or till edges are lightly browned and cookies are set. Remove cookies to wire racks; cool. Makes 42 cookies.

**Note:** Add some color to these cookies by drizzling them with melted *pastel candy coating, confectioner's coating* or *almond bark*. Stir ½ teaspoon *shortening* into the mixture for easy drizzling.

# CANDY-CANE SWIRL COOKIES

iana McMillen, a food editor for *Midwest Living*® magazine, has been baking cookies since she was a child. She especially likes these minty slice-and-bake treats because they add color to any cookie tray.

½ cup shortening
½ cup butter
3 cups all-purpose flour
1 cup sugar
1 egg
2 tablespoons milk
1 teaspoon vanilla
½ teaspoon baking soda
¼ teaspoon salt
¾ teaspoon peppermint extract
½ teaspoon red food coloring

1 In a large mixing bowl, beat shortening and butter with electric mixer about 30 seconds or till softened.

2 Add about *1½ cups* of the flour, the sugar, egg, milk, vanilla, baking soda and salt to butter mixture. Beat with electric mixer till thoroughly combined, scraping sides of bowl occasionally. Beat or stir in the remaining flour.

3 Divide dough in half. Set aside *one portion*. To the remaining portion, add the peppermint extract and the food coloring; knead till thoroughly combined.

4 To shape dough, separately roll out each portion of dough between 2 sheets of waxed paper to form each into a 12×11-inch rectangle. Remove top sheets of waxed paper from plain and pink doughs. Invert plain dough on top of pink dough. Peel off top sheet of paper. Beginning from a long side, roll up the dough, jelly-roll style, removing bottom sheet of paper as you roll. Cut roll in half, crosswise. Wrap in plastic wrap and refrigerate for 4 to 24 hours.

5 Cut dough into ¼-inch-thick slices. Place slices 2 inches apart on ungreased cookie sheets. Bake in a 375° oven for 8 to 10 minutes or till edges are firm and bottoms are lightly browned. Remove cookies to wire racks; cool. Makes about 60 cookies.

# DUTCH ALMOND BARS

ustomers indulge in these European-style sweets at the Till Midnight restaurant and bakery in Holland, Michigan. The buttery, rich bars will surely become a favorite at your house. (Pictured on next page on the upper left of plate.)

1 cup butter
¾ cup sugar
1 egg yolk
2 cups all-purpose flour
1 teaspoon ground
    cinnamon

¼ teaspoon baking soda
1 beaten egg white
½ cup sliced almonds
Powdered Sugar Drizzle
    (recipe follows;
    optional)

1 In a large mixing bowl, beat the butter with an electric mixer about 30 seconds or till softened. Add the sugar to butter mixture and beat till fluffy. Add the egg yolk and beat till thoroughly combined.

2 Stir together the flour, cinnamon and baking soda. Add to butter mixture; beat till just combined.

3 Place the dough in the center of a 15×10×1-inch baking pan. Spread the dough evenly in the pan.

4 Brush the top of dough with egg white and sprinkle with almonds, pressing almonds into the dough.

5 Bake in 350° oven for 15 to 18 minutes or till golden brown. Let stand in the baking pan for 5 minutes. Immediately cut into squares. Transfer squares to wire racks; cool. If you like, drizzle Powdered Sugar Drizzle over bars. Makes 36 bars.

**Powdered Sugar Drizzle:** In a mixing bowl, stir together 1 cup sifted *powdered sugar*, 1 tablespoon *milk* and ¼ teaspoon *vanilla*. Stir in more *milk, 1 teaspoon* at a time, till mixture is of drizzling consistency.

# SWEDISH SPRITZ COOKIES

wedish immigrant Ulla Olson, who lives in Rockford, Illinois, shares this easy recipe for her buttery pressed cookies. They come from her native land. (Pictured on next page on the lower half and upper right of plate.)

1 cup butter
½ cup sugar
1 egg yolk

1 teaspoon almond extract
2½ cups all-purpose flour

1 In a mixing bowl, beat the butter and sugar with an electric mixer till mixture is fluffy. Add egg yolk and almond extract and beat well. Beat or stir in the flour.

2 Force the *unchilled* dough through a cookie press onto ungreased cookie sheets.*

3 Bake in a 375° oven for 8 to 10 minutes or till the edges are firm, but not brown. Remove cookies to wire racks; cool. Makes about 60 cookies.

**Nutty Spritz Cookies:** Prepare Swedish Spritz Cookies, except stir in ½ cup finely ground *waluts* or *pecans* with the flour. (If you like, to bring out their flavor, toast the nuts before grinding. Place the nuts in a small skillet. Cook over medium heat, stirring often, for 5 to 7 minutes or till golden brown.)

**Chocolate Spritz Cookies:** Prepare Swedish Spritz Cookies, except instead of ½ cup sugar, stir in ¾ cup *sugar* and ¼ cup *unsweetened cocoa powder*. Decrease the flour to 2¼ *cups*. Beat or stir in the flour.

**Marbled Spritz Cookies:** Prepare 1 recipe Swedish Spritz Cookies and 1 recipe Chocolate Spritz Cookies. Alternately place about ¼ *cup each* of chocolate dough and white dough in cookie press.

**\*Note:** If you like, sprinkle cookies with *colored sugar* or *small decorative candies* before baking.

DUTCH ALMOND BARS AND
SWEDISH SPRITZ COOKIES

# FANCY RASPBERRY RIBBONS

The recipe for these festive raspberry-flavored cookies comes from the archives of the historic Alexander Ramsey House in St. Paul, Minnesota. You can vary the flavor to your liking by using the fruit jam or jelly of your choice.

1 cup butter, softened
2½ cups all-purpose flour
½ cup sugar
1 slightly beaten egg
1 teaspoon vanilla

¼ teaspoon salt
Raspberry jam or jelly
Almond Glaze (recipe follows)

1 In a mixing bowl, beat the butter with an electric mixer about 30 seconds or till softened. Add about *half* of the flour, the sugar, egg, vanilla and salt. Beat with electric mixer till thoroughly combined.

2 Beat or stir in the remaining flour till dough forms a ball. Gather dough into a ball and knead slightly. Divide the dough into 8 equal portions.

3 On a lightly floured surface, roll each portion of dough into a 9-inch-long rope. Place the ropes on ungreased cookie sheets about 2 inches apart. With the side of your finger or the handle of a wooden spoon, press a long groove down length of each rope.

4 Bake in a 375° oven for 10 minutes. Spoon jam or jelly into grooves and bake about 5 minutes more or till edges begin to brown slightly.

5 Cool on cookie sheets for 5 minutes. Using a large spatula, remove to a cutting board.

6 Drizzle Almond Glaze over hot cookies. Cut ropes into 1-inch-long pieces. Cool on wire racks. Makes 72 cookies.

**Almond Glaze:** In a bowl, mix ¾ cup sifted *powdered sugar* and ¼ teaspoon *almond extract*. Stir in 3 to 4 teaspoons *milk* till mixture is of drizzling consistency.

# DECADENT CHOCOLATE-FILLED BARS

 When Janet Summers of McPherson, Kansas, is in the mood to bake, she whips up her "super-easy, super-delicious" chocolate bars. The gooey shortbreadlike bars have a baked-in chocolate filling.

1 cup butter
2 cups all-purpose flour
½ cup sugar
⅛ teaspoon salt
1 14-ounce can sweetened condensed milk

1 6-ounce package (1 cup) semisweet chocolate pieces
½ cup chopped walnuts
½ teaspoon vanilla

1 In a large mixing bowl, beat butter with an electric mixer about 30 seconds or till softened.

2 Add flour, sugar and salt; beat on low speed till combined. Press *two-thirds* of the mixture into the bottom of an ungreased 13×9×2-inch baking pan.

3 In a medium saucepan, combine the sweetened condensed milk and chocolate. Stir over low heat till chocolate melts and mixture is smooth. Remove from heat. Stir in walnuts and vanilla. Spread hot mixture over the crust. Dot with remaining butter mixture.

4 Bake in a 350° oven about 35 minutes or till golden brown. Cool in pan on wire rack. Cut into bars. Makes 48 bars.

# NORWEGIAN FINA-GRUBBER

These Old World almond-flavored cookies from Midwest baker Marion Lorenzin of Chicago, Illinois, are perfect for an open house, bridal or baby shower, holiday party or any festive occasion.

1⅓ cups all-purpose flour
⅓ cup sugar
⅔ cup butter
1 egg yolk
¼ to ½ teaspoon almond
   extract

1 beaten egg white
⅓ cup finely chopped
   almonds, toasted
2 tablespoons sugar

1 In a large mixing bowl, stir together the flour and the ⅓ cup sugar. Using a pastry blender, cut in butter till the mixture resembles coarse crumbs.

2 Stir together the egg yolk and almond extract. Add to the flour mixture, using your hands to combine. Form dough into a ball.

3 Divide dough into 8 equal portions. On a lightly floured surface, roll each portion of dough into a 10-inch-long rope (about ½ inch thick). Cut each rope into 2-inch-long pieces. Dip one side of each piece into egg white, then into nuts and, finally, into the 2 tablespoons sugar.

4 Place dough pieces, uncoated sides down, on greased cookie sheets. Bake in a 325° oven for 8 to 10 minutes or till the tops are just set, but not brown. Transfer cookies to wire racks; cool. Makes 40 cookies.

# DELICATE LEMON SNOWDROPS

These sandwich cookies disappear like melting snow when Rita Hatfield takes them to potlucks in Cisco, Illinois. And it's no wonder—they have an irresistible lemon flavor. The lemon curd filling gives them a special flair.

1 cup butter
½ cup sifted powdered sugar
1 teaspoon lemon flavoring
2 cups all-purpose flour
¼ teaspoon salt
⅔ cup sugar
1 tablespoon cornstarch

1 teaspoon finely shredded
   lemon peel
3 tablespoons lemon juice
1 beaten egg
1 tablespoon butter,
   softened

1 Beat the 1 cup butter with an electric mixer about 30 seconds or till softened. Add powdered sugar and lemon flavoring; beat well. Add flour and salt. Beat well. (If necessary, stir in remaining flour by hand.)

2 Shape into 1-inch balls. Place balls 2 inches apart on ungreased cookie sheets. Flatten to 2-inch circles with the bottom of a glass dipped in *sugar.** Bake in a 375° oven for 8 to 10 minutes or till edges are lightly browned. Remove cookies to wire racks; cool.

3 For filling, in a saucepan, stir together the ⅔ cup sugar and cornstarch. Stir in lemon peel and juice. Cook and stir over medium heat till mixture is thickened. Cook and stir for 2 minutes more. Gradually stir about *half* of the hot mixture into beaten egg. Return all of egg mixture to saucepan. Cook and stir for 2 minutes more; *don't boil*. Remove from heat. Stir in the 1 tablespoon butter. Cover surface with plastic wrap; refrigerate.

4 To assemble, spread the filling on the flat sides of *half* of the cookies, using about *1½ teaspoons* filling on each; top with the remaining cookies, flat sides down. Store cookies, covered, in the refrigerator. Makes about 24 cookies.

***Note:** To spruce up these treats, you can dip the glass in *colored sugar* before flattening the cookie dough.

# BEST PEACH PIE

Celebrate peach season and choose just-picked fruit at a farmers' market for this melt-in-your mouth peach pie, a favorite all across the Midwest. During the winter months, rely on frozen peach slices.

6 cups thinly sliced, peeled peaches or frozen unsweetened peach slices
Double-Crust Pastry (recipe below)
½ cup sugar
1½ tablespoons quick-cooking tapioca
½ teaspoon ground cinnamon
3 tablespoons finely chopped crystallized ginger (optional)
Milk
Sugar
Ground cinnamon

**1** If using frozen peaches, let the peaches stand at room temperature for 15 to 30 minutes or till partially thawed, but still icy.

**2** Meanwhile, prepare Double-Crust Pastry as directed; divide pastry in half. Roll out *one half* of the pastry to a 12-inch circle. Line a 9-inch pie plate with pastry. For top crust, roll out remaining pastry to a 12-inch circle. Cover; set aside.

**3** In a large bowl, combine the ½ cup sugar, the tapioca and the ½ teaspoon cinnamon. If you like, stir in the crystallized ginger. Add the peaches, tossing to coat. Turn mixture into the pastry-lined pie plate.

**4** For top crust, follow directions in recipe below for a lattice top or for a regular top. Brush the crust with milk. (If you like, cut shapes, such as leaves, from pastry trimmings; press them into crust.) Sprinkle crust with additional sugar and cinnamon.

**5** Cover edge with foil to prevent overbrowning. Bake in a 375° oven for 50 minutes. Remove foil; bake for 20 to 25 minutes more or till golden brown. Cool on wire rack. Makes 8 servings.

# DOUBLE-CRUST PASTRY

This melt-in-your-mouth, old-fashioned pastry is ideal for making double-crust or lattice-top pies and dumplings. Pick from either the lattice or regular top crust directions. (For a single-crust pie, see recipe, page 21.)

2 cups all-purpose flour
½ teaspoon salt
⅔ cup shortening
6 to 7 tablespoons cold water

**1** In a large mixing bowl, stir together the flour and salt. Using a pastry blender, cut in the shortening till the pieces are the size of small peas.

**2** Sprinkle *1 tablespoon* of the water over part of the flour mixture; gently toss with a fork. Push moistened dough to the sides of the bowl. Repeat with remaining water till all is moistened. Proceed as directed in individual recipes. (Or, for a lattice or regular top, follow directions at right.)

**Lattice Top:** Trim bottom pastry to ½ inch beyond edge of pie plate. Cut 12-inch pastry circle into ½-inch-wide strips. To weave lattice, lay *half* of the pastry strips atop peach mixture at 1-inch intervals. Fold alternate pastry strips back halfway. Place another pastry strip in the center across the strips already in place. Unfold folded strips; fold back remaining strips. Place another pastry strip parallel to strip in center. Repeat weaving steps till lattice covers filling. Press ends of strips into rim of crust. Fold bottom pastry over strips. Seal and flute the edge. If you like, roll out pastry scraps and cut into decorative shapes.

**Regular Top:** Trim bottom pastry even with edge of pie plate. Cut slits in 12-inch pastry circle to allow steam to escape. Place top crust over filling. Trim top crust ½ inch beyond edge of pie plate. Fold top crust under bottom crust; flute edge.

# CRANBERRY-RASPBERRY PIE

 edges of this sweet-tart, rosy-colored pie bring oohs and aahs when they're served at The First Grade restaurant in Grand Rapids, Minnesota. Earn your own rounds of approval by serving it at your next special gathering.

Double-Crust Pastry
   (recipe page 64)
1½ cups frozen loose-pack
   red raspberries, thawed
¼ cup quick-cooking tapioca
1 12-ounce package
   (3 cups) cranberries,
   halved or coarsely
   chopped

2¼ cups sugar
½ teaspoon almond extract
   Milk
   Sugar
   Ice cream or sweetened
   whipped cream
   (optional)

1 Prepare Double-Crust Pastry as directed; divide pastry in half. Roll out *one half* to a 12-inch circle. Line a 9-inch pie plate with pastry. Trim pastry even with edge of pie plate. For the top crust, roll out the remaining pastry to a 12-inch circle. Cut slits or star shapes into the top crust to let steam escape.

2 In a large mixing bowl, combine the *undrained* raspberries and tapioca. Add cranberries, the 2¼ cups sugar and almond extract. Stir mixture till well combined. Let stand at room temperature 15 minutes.

3 Turn fruit mixture into pastry-lined pie plate. Place top crust over fruit mixture. Trim top crust ½ inch beyond edge of pie plate. Fold top crust under bottom crust; flute edge. Brush with milk.

4 Roll out dough scraps. With a small star-shaped cookie cutter, cut stars from pastry. Arrange on top crust so that each piece will have stars. Brush cutouts with milk. Sprinkle top with sugar. Cover edge with foil to prevent overbrowning.

5 Bake in a 375° oven for 30 minutes. Remove foil; bake for 20 to 30 minutes more or till top crust is golden brown and juices are clear. If you like, serve with ice cream or sweetened whipped cream. Serves 8.

# CLIFTON MILL CHOCOLATE-PECAN PIE

 n the restaurant at historic Clifton Mill near Yellow Springs, Ohio, diners sample many temptations, including this rich pecan pie. The added chocolate makes ordinary pecan pie a chocolate-lover's dream come true.

Single-Crust Pastry
   (recipe page 21)
3 tablespoons butter
2 ounces unsweetened
   chocolate

3 eggs
1 cup dark corn syrup
¾ cup sugar
1 teaspoon vanilla
1 cup pecan halves

1 Prepare Single-Crust Pastry as directed. Set aside. In a medium saucepan, melt butter and chocolate over low heat, stirring constantly. Cool slightly.

2 In a large mixing bowl, beat together the eggs, corn syrup, sugar and vanilla. Add melted chocolate mixture; beat well. Stir in pecans.

3 Turn pecan mixture into pastry-lined pie plate. Cover edge with foil to prevent overbrowning. Bake in a 375° oven for 20 minutes. Remove foil; bake for 20 to 30 minutes more or till a knife inserted near the center comes out clean. Cool on wire rack. Cover; store in refrigerator. Makes 8 servings.

# REUNION SWEET POTATO PIE

The descendants of the late Curtis Mae McDaniel and her husband, Robert, of Cincinnati, Ohio, gather every year for their family reunion. This pie makes a mandatory appearance at each McDaniel reunion.

2 large sweet potatoes (about 1½ pounds)
½ cup shortening
1 cup all-purpose flour
2 to 4 tablespoons cold water
1 cup butter, softened
1½ cups sugar

1 12-ounce can (1½ cups) evaporated milk
½ to 1 teaspoon ground nutmeg
½ teaspoon vanilla
¼ teaspoon salt
3 beaten eggs
Whipped cream (optional)

**1** In a covered saucepan, cook the sweet potatoes in *boiling water* for 30 to 40 minutes or till tender. (Or, pierce sweet potatoes and microwave on 100% power [high] for 8 to 10 minutes or till the potatoes are tender.) Cool.

**2** Meanwhile, for the pastry, using a pastry blender, cut shortening into flour till mixture resembles coarse crumbs. Sprinkle *1 tablespoon* of the water over part of the flour mixture; gently toss with a fork. Push moistened dough to the sides of the bowl. Repeat with remaining water till all is moistened. Form the dough into a ball. Cover and refrigerate for 20 to 30 minutes for easier handling.

**3** Roll out pastry, forming a 13-inch circle. Wrap around rolling pin. Unroll onto a 10-inch pie plate. Ease the pastry into the pie plate, being careful not to stretch the pastry. Trim pastry to ½ inch beyond edge of pie plate. Fold pastry under; flute edge. Partially bake in a 450° oven for 5 minutes. Cool slightly on wire rack. Reduce the oven temperature to 375°.

**4** Meanwhile, drain and peel sweet potatoes (or scrape peel from sweet potatoes). Press sweet potatoes through a colander into a bowl. (Or, place sweet potatoes in bowl. Mash with a potato masher or beat with an electric mixer on low speed.) Mix in butter till melted and thoroughly combined.

**5** Add sugar, evaporated milk, nutmeg, vanilla, salt and eggs. Press through the colander again or beat with an electric mixer till smooth.

**6** Place pastry-lined pie plate on oven rack; spoon sweet potato mixture into pie plate. Cover edge with foil to prevent overbrowning. Bake in a 375° oven for 25 minutes. Remove foil; bake for 20 to 25 minutes more or till knife inserted near center comes out clean. Cool on wire rack. Cover; store in refrigerator. If you like, serve with whipped cream. Makes 8 servings.

# It's All in the Rolling Pin

Many Midwest bakers attribute their pastry-making prowess to "trusty" rolling pins that they've used for years. While the rolling pins themselves may not guarantee perfect pie crusts, the fact that the cooks are comfortable using them does. Choosing the right rolling pin is much like selecting the right baseball bat or bowling ball—the rolling pin needs to fit your hands. For most uses, such as rolling out pastry or cookie dough, all-purpose wooden pins are ideal. For specialty uses, such as rolling out pasta or bread dough, you might want to consider marble, hollow or tapered French rolling pins. Some cooks even prefer smooth wooden dowels because they have no handles to get in the way.

# CHOCOLATE-RASPBERRY FUDGE TART

Chef/owner Jackie Shen of Jackie's restaurant in Chicago, Illinois, tops this chocolate creation with melted raspberry jam and raspberries. Now you don't have to travel to the Windy City to taste it because Jackie shares her recipe here.

Single-Crust Pastry
 (recipe page 21)
½ cup butter
4 ounces semisweet
 chocolate, cut up
¾ cup sugar
2 eggs
1 egg yolk

½ teaspoon vanilla
¼ cup half-and-half or light
 cream
2 tablespoons raspberry
 jam, melted
Raspberry jam, melted
 (optional)
Fresh raspberries
 (optional)

**1** Prepare and roll out Single-Crust Pastry as directed. Ease pastry into a 9-inch tart pan (with removable bottom) or a 9-inch pie plate. Trim edge if using a tart pan or, if using a pie plate, flute edge. Line the pastry with a double thickness of heavy foil. Bake in a 450° oven for 10 minutes. Remove the foil. Reduce oven temperature to 325°.

**2** In a heavy medium saucepan, melt the butter and chocolate over low heat, stirring constantly. Stir in the sugar, eggs, egg yolk and vanilla till smooth. Stir in the half-and-half or light cream. Turn the chocolate mixture into the pastry-lined tart pan or pie plate.

**3** Bake in a 325° oven for 25 to 30 minutes or till the center is nearly set when you shake it. Cool completely on a wire rack. Remove rim from tart pan.

**4** Brush the cooled tart with 2 tablespoons melted raspberry jam. Cover; store in refrigerator.

**5** If you like, drizzle additional melted raspberry jam over each serving and top with fresh raspberries. Makes 8 servings.

---

# SUMMERTIME CHOOSE-A-FRUIT TART

At The Inn at Cedar Falls near Logan, Ohio, Ellen Grinsfelder gathers the best fruit of the season for this spiced, streusel-topped tart. We've only given a few fruit suggestions here. The choices, however, are many.

1 cup all-purpose flour
3 tablespoons sugar
¼ teaspoon baking powder
¼ cup cold butter
1 egg
½ teaspoon almond extract
3 cups fresh fruit
 (blueberries, peeled and
 sliced apples and/or
 peeled and sliced
 peaches)

1 tablespoon lemon juice
2 tablespoons sugar
 (optional)
½ cup all-purpose flour
½ cup sugar
⅛ teaspoon ground
 cinnamon
⅛ teaspoon ground nutmeg
6 tablespoons butter
 Whipped cream or ice
 cream (optional)

**1** Grease a 9-inch tart pan (with removable bottom) or a 9-inch pie plate. Set aside. In a food processor, place the 1 cup flour, the 3 tablespoons sugar and the baking powder. Process till combined.* Add the ¼ cup cold butter. Process till mixture resembles fine crumbs. Add the egg and the almond extract. Process the mixture till the dough forms a ball. With floured hands, press dough onto the bottom and up the sides of the prepared tart pan or pie plate.

**2** In a medium bowl, toss together the fruit and lemon juice. If you like, add the 2 tablespoons sugar and toss. Turn into pastry-lined tart pan or pie plate.

**3** Combine the ½ cup flour, ½ cup sugar, cinnamon and nutmeg. Using a pastry blender, cut in the 6 tablespoons butter till crumbly. Sprinkle over fruit.

**4** Cover edge with foil to prevent overbrowning. Bake in a 350° oven for 35 to 40 minutes or till golden brown. Cool on a wire rack. If you like, serve with whipped cream or ice cream. Makes 8 servings.

***Note:** If you don't have a food processor, use a pastry blender to cut in the butter. Then, stir in the egg and almond extract with a fork.

SUMMERTIME
CHOOSE-A-FRUIT TART

# CHERRY-VANILLA SPIRAL CAKE

ed cherry sauce lends a festive touch to spirals of cake and vanilla filling. Convenience products make fast work of this dessert, which comes from the grandmother of Jerry Schmidt of Minneapolis, Minnesota.

| | |
|---|---|
| 1 4-serving-size package vanilla pudding mix* | 1 cup all-purpose flour |
| 5 eggs | ¼ teaspoon salt |
| ½ cup sugar | ½ cup sugar |
| 2 tablespoons lemon juice | Sifted powdered sugar |
| 1 tablespoon water | 1 21-ounce can cherry pie filling |

**1** Prepare pudding mix according to package directions; refrigerate. Separate eggs. In a medium mixing bowl, beat egg yolks with an electric mixer till lemon-colored. Beat in ½ cup sugar, lemon juice and water. Beat in flour and salt.

**2** Wash beaters thoroughly. In a large bowl, beat egg whites till soft peaks form. Gradually add ½ cup sugar, beating till stiff peaks form. Fold egg yolk mixture into egg white mixture.

**3** Grease a 15×10×1-inch baking pan; line pan with waxed paper and grease and flour the waxed paper. Turn batter into pan, spreading evenly.

**4** Bake in a 350° oven about 15 minutes or till cake springs back when touched lightly with your finger.

**5** Immediately loosen edges of cake from the pan and turn cake out onto a towel sprinkled with powdered sugar. Remove waxed paper. Roll up towel and cake together, jelly-roll style, starting from one of the short sides. Cool the cake on a wire rack.

**6** Unroll cake; remove towel. Spread cake with the pudding to within 1 inch of edges. Roll up from one of the short sides. Cover; store in refrigerator.**

**7** To serve, sprinkle the cake with powdered sugar. Top with the cherry pie filling. Makes 10 servings.

*Note: If you like, substitute 2 cups softened *ice cream* or *frozen yogurt* or 2 cups *homemade pudding* for the purchased pudding mix.

**Note: If you've filled the cake roll with ice cream or frozen yogurt, freeze it.

# Whipping Up Egg Whites

Quiz Heartland bakers who are famous for their feather-light cakes, and they'll tell you that success depends on beating the egg whites correctly. Here are some of their pointers:

♦ The best time to separate eggs is when the eggs are cold. Be careful not to get even a speck of yolk into the whites. Place the whites in a glass or metal bowl, not a plastic one. Be sure the bowl and the beaters from your mixer are completely clean. (Fat from egg yolk or any greasy residue on utensils or plastic bowls will cause the egg whites to lose volume when you beat them.)

♦ For the greatest volume, let egg whites stand at room temperature about 30 minutes to warm up.

♦ Beat the egg whites with an electric mixer on medium to high speed till the tips curl when you lift the beaters. This is the soft-peak stage. Then, gradually add the sugar till stiff peaks form. At this stage, the tips of the peaks will stand up straight when you lift the beaters.

# DARK CHOCOLATE-NUT CAKE

Sharon Winstein from St. Louis, Missouri, serves this cake at Passover. But it's so delicious, there's no reason to wait for a holiday to bake this rich, flourless cake. Follow the tips below to ensure your success with making flourless cakes.

10 to 12 eggs
3 ounces unsweetened chocolate
½ cup semisweet chocolate pieces
⅔ cup sugar
2 cups ground almonds
¾ teaspoon pure vanilla
¼ teaspoon almond extract
¼ cup sugar
Dark Chocolate Glaze (recipe follows)

1 Separate eggs (you should have 1½ cups whites). Place whites in a very large bowl. Place yolks in another large bowl. Let separated eggs stand, covered, at room temperature 30 minutes.

2 Meanwhile, in a heavy small saucepan, partially melt unsweetened chocolate and semisweet chocolate pieces over low heat, stirring constantly. Turn off heat and stir till smooth.

3 Cut a waxed-paper liner for the bottom of a 10-inch tube pan, cutting it ½ inch wider than the pan and cutting the center hole slightly larger than the tube. Grease pan thoroughly. Place liner in pan and grease and flour liner.

4 Beat egg yolks with an electric mixer on high speed about 4 minutes or till thick and lemon-colored. Add the ⅔ cup sugar, beating till very thick. Stir in the melted chocolate and ground nuts.

5 Wash the beaters thoroughly. Beat the egg whites with vanilla and almond extract till foamy. Gradually add the ¼ cup sugar, beating till soft peaks form (tips curl).

6 Stir about *2 cups* of the beaten egg whites into the yolk mixture to lighten. Add to the remaining egg white mixture and fold together to combine. Turn batter into prepared pan.

7 Bake in a 350° oven for 50 to 55 minutes or till top springs back when touched lightly with your finger. Run a knife around the edge of the pan and center to loosen. Cool in pan for 1 hour. (Cake may dip slightly in center.) Invert onto cake plate. Remove waxed paper. Spread Dark Chocolate Glaze over top and sides of cake. Makes 10 to 15 servings.

**Dark Chocolate Glaze:** In a heavy small saucepan or skillet, melt 1 cup *semisweet chocolate pieces* over low heat, stirring constantly. Remove from heat and stir in 1 teaspoon *butter*. In a small bowl, dissolve ¼ teaspoon *instant coffee crystals* in 1 tablespoon *hot water*. Stir in 3 tablespoons *dairy sour cream* and ¼ teaspoon *maple flavoring*. Add sour cream mixture to chocolate, stirring till smooth and shiny. Makes ¾ cup.

## Perfect Flourless Cakes

Some flourless cakes or tortes use nuts in place of all or some of the all-purpose flour. For these recipes, it is important to use *very fine* and *dry* ground nuts. Grinding nuts to the right stage can be tricky because nuts will form a paste if ground too much. To prevent this, grind the nuts in small batches with a food grinder, blender or food processor. If using a blender or food processor, try adding 1 tablespoon of sugar from the recipe for *each* cup of nuts when processing, then quickly start and stop the appliance for better control over the fineness of the ground nuts.

# LEMON CREAM DESSERT CAKE

**S**tart with a cake mix to simplify making this light and citrusy creation. The cake is layered with a lemony cream cheese frosting that is hard to resist. Diana Breedlove of Ashtabula, Ohio, shares this crowd pleaser so you can make it, too.

| | |
|---|---|
| 1 package 2-layer-size white cake mix | 2 tablespoons finely shredded lemon peel |
| 1 cup water | 3 tablespoons lemon juice |
| ⅓ cup cooking oil | 2 to 3 drops yellow food coloring |
| 3 egg whites | Creamy Lemon Frosting (recipe follows) |
| 3 egg yolks | |

**1** Grease and flour a 10-inch tube pan. Set aside. In a large mixing bowl, beat cake mix, water, oil and egg whites with an electric mixer on low speed till moistened. Beat the mixture for 2 minutes on high speed. Set aside *2 cups* of the batter.

**2** In a small bowl, beat egg yolks on high speed for 2 minutes. Stir in the 2 cups reserved batter, the lemon peel, lemon juice and food coloring.

**3** Layer batters alternately in prepared pan, beginning and ending with yellow batter. Using a narrow spatula, gently swirl through batters to marble. Bake in a 350° oven about 45 minutes or till wooden toothpick inserted in center comes out clean. Cool on wire rack for 15 minutes; remove from pan and cool completely.

**4** To assemble cake, cut cake horizontally into three layers. Spread some of the Creamy Lemon Frosting between layers. Frost entire cake with remaining frosting. Makes 12 servings.

**Creamy Lemon Frosting:** In a large mixing bowl, beat 1 cup sifted *powdered sugar* and one 8-ounce package *cream cheese* (softened) till smooth. Fold in one 8-ounce container *frozen whipped dessert topping*, thawed. In a small mixing bowl, beat one 4-serving-size package *instant vanilla pudding mix* and 1 cup *milk* with electric mixer on low speed for 2 minutes; stir in 1 tablespoon finely shredded *lemon peel*. Fold the pudding into the cream cheese mixture.

## Cutting Cake Layers with Ease

To assemble Lemon-Cream Dessert Cake, follow these simple directions for slicing the cake into layers. Start by using a ruler to measure the height of the cake and insert a toothpick (horizontally) one-third of the way up from the bottom of the cake and another toothpick two-thirds of the way up from the bottom. Repeat this measuring process at about 2-inch intervals until you've gone completely around the cake. Then, using the toothpicks as guides, slice the cake into three layers with a long, serrated knife.

LEMON CREAM
DESSERT CAKE

# ANGIE'S PUMPKIN ROLL

iners at Lucretia's restaurant in Ste. Genevieve, Missouri, choose from a dessert tray of sweets, including this pumpkin sensation. Each slice has a decorative swirl of decadent Cream Cheese Filling.

1 cup sugar
¾ cup packaged biscuit mix
1 teaspoon pumpkin pie
   spice
1 teaspoon ground
   cinnamon
½ teaspoon ground nutmeg

⅔ cup canned pumpkin
3 eggs
1 cup finely chopped nuts
   Sifted powdered sugar
   Cream Cheese Filling
   (recipe follows)

1 Grease a 15×10×1-inch baking pan. Line pan with waxed paper. Lightly grease waxed paper. Set aside.

2 In a large bowl, stir together sugar, biscuit mix, pumpkin pie spice, cinnamon and nutmeg. In a medium bowl, stir together the pumpkin and eggs. Add pumpkin mixture to sugar mixture; stir till combined. Spread evenly into prepared pan. Sprinkle with nuts.

3 Bake in a 375° oven for 13 to 15 minutes or till wooden toothpick inserted in the center comes out clean. Immediately loosen edges of cake from pan and turn cake out onto a towel dusted with powdered sugar. Remove waxed paper. Roll up towel and cake together, jelly-roll style, starting from one of the short sides. Cool the cake on a wire rack.

4 Unroll cake and remove the towel. Spread cake with Cream Cheese Filling to within 1 inch of edges. Roll up cake from one of the short sides. Cover and store in the refrigerator. Makes 8 servings.

**Cream Cheese Filling:** In a small mixing bowl, beat one 8-ounce package *cream cheese* (softened), 6 tablespoons *butter* and 1 teaspoon *vanilla* till light and fluffy. Gradually add 1 cup sifted *powdered sugar;* beat well.

# ORANGE-SLICE GUMDROP CAKE

ary E. Francis often bakes this moist, sweet cake as a gift for her lucky neighbors and church friends in Rapid City, South Dakota. Share this special cake, filled with dates, coconut and nuts, with your own friends.

1 cup butter
4 eggs
1 pound orange
   slice-shaped gumdrops,
   cut up (3 cups)
½ cup all-purpose flour
2 cups sugar
3 cups all-purpose flour

1 cup buttermilk
1 8-ounce package pitted
   dates, cut up
1 7-ounce package flaked
   coconut
2 cups chopped nuts
   Orange Glaze (recipe
   follows)

1 Let butter and eggs stand at room temperature for 30 minutes. Combine gumdrops and the ½ cup flour. Grease and flour two 9×5×3-inch loaf pans; line with waxed paper. Set aside.

2 In an extra-large bowl, beat butter with an electric mixer 30 seconds or till softened. Gradually add sugar, beating till combined. Add eggs, one at a time, beating after each addition, scraping bowl frequently. Add the 3 cups flour and buttermilk alternately to egg mixture; beat after each addition. Fold in dates, coconut and nuts. Fold in gumdrop mixture.

3 Spread batter evenly into prepared pans. Bake in a 300° oven about 1 hour and 40 minutes or till a wooden toothpick inserted in center comes out clean.

4 Pour Orange Glaze over the hot cakes. Cool in pans on wire racks for 20 minutes. Remove from pans; remove waxed paper. Cool completely. Wrap each cake in plastic wrap. Store in refrigerator for up to 4 weeks. To serve, bring to room temperature. Serves 16 to 20.

**Orange Glaze:** In a small bowl, stir together 2 cups sifted *powdered sugar* and ½ cup *orange juice* till smooth.

# TAPAWINGO'S PEAR AND GINGER CAKE

Most diners at Pete Peterson's Tapawingo restaurant in Ellsworth, Michigan, order dessert. This flavorful ginger cake is one obvious reason why. The Pear Sauce makes it an elegant dessert to make for guests.

½ cup unsalted butter or
　　regular butter
½ cup packed brown sugar
2 eggs
¼ cup molasses
1 tablespoon grated fresh
　　gingerroot
1½ cups all-purpose flour
1 teaspoon baking soda
½ teaspoon salt
½ teaspoon ground allspice

¼ teaspoon ground cloves
¼ teaspoon ground nutmeg
⅔ cup buttermilk or sour
　　milk*
1 medium pear (such as
　　Anjou or Bartlett),
　　peeled and thinly sliced
Sifted powdered sugar
Pear Sauce (recipe
　　follows)

1 Butter and lightly flour a 2-quart square (8×8×2-inch) baking dish. Set aside.

2 In a large mixing bowl, beat the ½ cup butter with an electric mixer about 30 seconds or till softened.

3 Add the brown sugar and beat till fluffy. Add the eggs, one at a time, beating well after each addition. Beat in the molasses and gingerroot.

4 In a bowl, stir together 1½ cups flour, baking soda, salt, allspice, cloves and nutmeg. Add flour mixture and buttermilk alternately to beaten mixture, beating on low speed after each addition till just combined.

5 Fold in the sliced pear. Spread batter in prepared dish. Bake in a 350° oven for 35 to 40 minutes or till a wooden toothpick inserted in center comes out clean. Cool in pan on wire rack.

6 To serve, cut the cake into squares. Dust the squares with powdered sugar and drizzle with Pear Sauce. Makes 9 to 12 servings.

**Pear Sauce:** Using a vegetable peeler, remove only the yellow peel from half a *lemon*. In a medium saucepan, combine the lemon peel, 2 tablespoons *lemon juice*, 1 cup *water* and ¼ cup *sugar*. Cook over medium heat till sugar dissolves.

Peel, core and quarter four 8-ounce *Anjou* or *Bartlett pears*. Add the pears to the sugar mixture. Cook the mixture, uncovered, about 12 minutes or till the pears are tender. Using a slotted spoon, remove pears from saucepan. Place pears in a blender container or a food processor bowl. Set aside.

Cook the sugar mixture in saucepan till it's reduced by *half*. Remove and discard the lemon peel. Pour the sugar mixture into the blender container or food processor bowl. Cover; blend or process till smooth. Stir in 2 tablespoons *Pear William liqueur* or *cognac*. Serve warm with cake.

**\*Note:** To make sour milk, place 2 teaspoons *lemon juice* in a glass measuring cup. Pour in enough *milk* to make ⅔ cup liquid. Stir and let stand for 5 minutes.

# Getting the Most from Gingeroot

Fresh gingerroot adds a delicious spice flavor to all types of dishes—both savory and sweet. You'll find the fresh root in the produce section of your supermarket. Grate the ginger, peel and all, with a ginger grater or fine shredder. To store the rest of the root for a few days, wrap it in a paper towel and refrigerate it. To store gingerroot for several months, freeze the unpeeled root in a moisture- and vapor-proof bag. Then, grate or cut off what you need from the frozen root.

# CHEERY MINT-CHOCOLATE CHEESECAKE

Crème de menthe lends a pale green accent and a hint of refreshing mint to this cheesecake from The Granville Inn in Granville, Ohio. The chocolate triangles aren't a must, of course, but they add a festive touch to the cake.

| | |
|---|---|
| **2 cups graham cracker crumbs** | **2 teaspoons vanilla** |
| **½ cup butter, melted** | **5 eggs** |
| **4 8-ounce packages cream cheese, softened** | **1 16-ounce carton dairy sour cream** |
| **1¼ cups sugar** | **⅓ cup sugar** |
| **¼ cup crème de menthe** | **1 cup milk chocolate pieces** |
| | **1 teaspoon shortening** |

**1** In a medium mixing bowl, combine graham cracker crumbs and melted butter. Press evenly on bottom and 2 inches up sides of a 10-inch springform pan.

**2** In a large mixing bowl, beat cream cheese, the 1¼ cups sugar, the crème de menthe and vanilla with an electric mixer on medium speed for 2 minutes. Add eggs all at once, beating on low speed till just combined. Turn mixture into prepared pan. Place on a shallow baking pan in oven.

**3** Bake in a 325° oven about 1 hour and 10 minutes or till center appears nearly set when you shake it.

**4** Stir together sour cream and the ⅓ cup sugar. Carefully spread over cheesecake. Bake for 10 minutes more. Cool on wire rack for 15 minutes. Loosen the cheesecake from sides of pan. Cool for 30 minutes more; remove sides of pan. Cool completely on wire rack. Cover and refrigerate for at least 4 hours.

**5** In a small saucepan, heat and stir chocolate and shortening over low heat till melted. Remove from heat. Pour onto a foil-lined baking sheet. Spread to a 7-inch circle. Cool for 5 minutes. If you like, use a cake comb to make ridges in chocolate. Cool till chocolate is firm enough to cut. Cut into 9 to 16 wedges.

**6** To serve, place the chocolate wedges on top of the cheesecake. Makes 9 to 16 servings.

# WHITE CHOCOLATE CHEESECAKE

From The Mandolin Inn, located in Dubuque, Iowa, this cheesecake is guaranteed to bring raves at any party. A drizzle of raspberry sauce over each serving makes a showy contrast against the creamy-white cake.

| | |
|---|---|
| **1 cup shortbread cookie crumbs (about 3 ounces)** | **1 6-ounce package white baking bar, melted and cooled** |
| **3 tablespoons finely chopped toasted slivered almonds** | **⅔ cup sugar** |
| **¼ cup butter, melted** | **3 eggs** |
| **2 8-ounce packages cream cheese, softened** | **⅔ cup dairy sour cream** |
| | **1 teaspoon vanilla** |
| | **Triple-Raspberry Sauce (recipe follows)** |

**1** In a small mixing bowl, combine cookie crumbs and almonds. Stir in melted butter. Press onto bottom of 8-inch springform pan.

**2** In a large bowl, beat cream cheese and cooled baking bar with an electric mixer till combined. Beat in sugar till fluffy. Add eggs, sour cream and vanilla; beat on low speed till just combined. Turn into prepared pan. Place on a shallow baking pan in oven. Bake in a 350° oven about 45 minutes or till center appears nearly set when you shake it.

**3** Cool on wire rack for 15 minutes. Loosen cake from sides of pan. Cool 30 minutes more; remove sides of pan. Cool completely. Cover; refrigerate at least 4 hours. Serve with Triple-Raspberry Sauce. Serves 8.

**Triple-Raspberry Sauce:** In a saucepan, melt one 10-ounce jar *seedless raspberry preserves* over low heat. Add 1 cup *fresh red raspberries* or *frozen loose-pack, lightly sweetened red raspberries*. Heat till sauce just simmers. Cool. If you like, stir in 1 to 2 tablespoons *raspberry liqueur*. Cover; refrigerate till serving time. To serve, spoon sauce over cheesecake. Makes 1⅔ cups.

CHEERY MINT-CHOCOLATE
CHEESECAKE

# JOANNE'S GERMAN CHOCOLATE CHEESECAKE

Try Wisconsonian Joanne Vanden Heuvel's luscious cheesecake at your next dinner party. It's guaranteed to bring you praise. Just like the cake that bears the name, this cheesecake has a luscious Coconut-Pecan Topping.

1 cup graham cracker
    crumbs
2 tablespoons sugar
⅓ cup butter, melted
¼ cup flaked coconut
¼ cup chopped pecans
4 ounces semisweet
    chocolate, chopped
3 8-ounce packages cream
    cheese, softened

¾ cup sugar
½ cup dairy sour cream
2 teaspoons vanilla
2 tablespoons all-purpose
    flour
3 eggs
    Coconut-Pecan Topping
    (recipe follows)

**1** For crust, in a medium mixing bowl, combine the graham cracker crumbs, the 2 tablespoons sugar, melted butter, coconut and pecans. Press evenly into bottom and ½ inch up sides of a 9-inch springform pan. Bake in a 350° oven for 8 to 10 minutes. Cool slightly. Increase oven temperature to 375°.

**2** In a saucepan, melt the chocolate over low heat, stirring constantly. Remove from heat; cool.

**3** For filling, in a large bowl, beat the cream cheese, the ¾ cup sugar, the sour cream and vanilla with an electric mixer till thoroughly combined. Add the flour and beat well. Add the eggs and cooled chocolate all at once; beat on low speed till just combined.

**4** Turn filling into cooled crust. Place on shallow baking pan in oven. Bake in a 375° oven for 45 to 50 minutes or till center appears nearly set when shaken. Cool on wire rack 15 minutes. Loosen cake from sides of pan. Cool 30 minutes more; remove sides of pan. Cool completely on wire rack.

**5** Spread Coconut-Pecan Topping over cheesecake. Cover; refrigerate for 3 to 24 hours. Serves 12 to 14.

**Coconut-Pecan Topping:** In a small saucepan, melt ½ cup *butter*. Stir in ¼ cup packed *brown sugar*, 2 tablespoons *half-and-half* or *light cream* and 2 tablespoons *light corn syrup*. Cook and stir over medium heat till bubbly. Stir in 1 cup *flaked coconut*, ½ cup chopped *pecans* and 1 teaspoon *vanilla*. Remove from heat; cool for 5 minutes.

# Company-Perfect Cheesecake

The Midwest is cheesecake country—almost every restaurant or home cook has a cherished recipe. For creamy cheesecakes with no large cracks follow these simple guidelines:

♦ Beat the batter gently. Overbeating can cause the cheesecake to puff up, then fall and crack.

♦ To tell if a cheesecake is baked, gently shake the pan rather than inserting a knife. The center should appear nearly set. (If you test with a knife, the slit may turn into a crack.) A 1-inch portion in the center may jiggle slightly when the cheesecake is done.

♦ Follow the directions for cooling *exactly*. Loosen the crust from the sides of the pan when specified, otherwise the cheesecake may pull away from the sides of the pan and crack.

# DECADENT HAZELNUT CHEESECAKE

It's elegant and delicious—the perfect meal finale. Hazelnut liqueur and hazelnuts make this cheesecake a popular choice at the Montague Inn in Saginaw, Michigan. If you like, substitute almond liqueur and almonds for the hazelnut liqueur and hazelnuts.

1 cup ground toasted
  hazelnuts (filberts)
2 tablespoons butter,
  melted
4 8-ounce packages cream
  cheese
1¼ cups sugar
2 teaspoons vanilla

½ teaspoon almond extract
5 eggs
¼ cup hazelnut liqueur
⅔ cup chopped toasted
  hazelnuts (filberts)
1 cup whipping cream
2 tablespoons hazelnut
  liqueur

1 In a medium mixing bowl, stir together the ground hazelnuts and the melted butter. Press the mixture onto the bottom of a 9-inch springform pan.

2 In a large bowl, combine the cream cheese, sugar, vanilla and almond extract; beat with an electric mixer till fluffy. Add eggs and beat on low speed till just combined. Stir in the ¼ cup hazelnut liqueur and the chopped hazelnuts. Turn into prepared pan. Place on shallow baking pan in oven.

3 Bake in a 350° oven about 1 hour or till center appears nearly set when you shake it. Cool on wire rack for 15 minutes. Loosen cheesecake from sides of pan. Cool for 30 minutes more; remove the sides of the pan. Cool completely on wire rack. Cover and refrigerate for at least 4 hours.

4 In a chilled mixing bowl, beat the whipping cream and the 2 tablespoons hazelnut liqueur with electric mixer till soft peaks form (tips curl). Serve whipped cream with the cheesecake. Makes 16 servings.

# AMARETTO CHEESECAKE

Order a slice of this regal cheesecake in the elegant dining room of the Pere Marquette Lodge near Grafton, Illinois. Or, lucky you, now you can savor it without leaving your house because they've shared the recipe here.

1 cup sliced almonds,
  toasted and finely
  chopped
1 cup graham cracker
  crumbs
⅓ cup butter, melted

4 8-ounce packages cream
  cheese, softened
2 cups sugar
¼ teaspoon almond extract
3 eggs
¼ cup amaretto liqueur or
  milk

1 For crust, in a medium mixing bowl, stir together the chopped almonds, graham cracker crumbs and melted butter. Press evenly 2 inches up the sides and into the bottom of a 9-inch springform pan.* Place in a shallow baking pan. Set aside.

2 For filling, in a large mixing bowl, beat cream cheese, sugar and almond extract with electric mixer till thoroughly combined.

3 Add eggs all at once; beat on low speed till just combined. Don't overbeat the mixture. Beat in the amaretto or the milk till just combined.

4 Turn filling into crust. Place on shallow baking pan in oven. Bake in a 350° oven for 60 to 65 minutes or till center appears nearly set when you shake it. Cool on wire rack for 10 minutes. Loosen cheesecake from sides of pan. Cool for 30 minutes more; remove the sides of the pan. Cover; refrigerate for 4 to 24 hours. Makes 14 to 16 servings.

*Note: When pressing the crust into the pan, start with the sides first, then use the remaining crumbs for the bottom.

# BLACK FOREST CREAM PUFFS

 chocolate drizzle completes these cherry-filled cream puffs, named for the chocolate-cherry cake from Karl Ratzsch's restaurant in Milwaukee, Wisconsin. Crown them with whipped cream.

½ cup milk
½ cup water
½ cup butter
1 cup all-purpose flour
5 eggs
5 cups frozen,
    unsweetened, pitted
    tart red cherries,
    thawed (about
    20 ounces)
1 cup sugar

¼ cup cornstarch
¼ cup kirsch (black cherry
    liqueur) or orange juice
3 drops red food coloring
1 tablespoon vanilla
2 ounces semisweet
    chocolate, melted and
    cooled
Sweetened whipped
    cream

**1** For cream puffs, in a medium saucepan, combine milk, water and butter. Bring to boiling. Add the flour all at once, stirring vigorously. Cook and stir till mixture forms a ball that doesn't separate. Remove the saucepan from heat. Cool the cream puff mixture for 5 minutes. Add eggs, one at a time, beating with a wooden spoon after each addition till smooth.

**2** Drop dough by a heaping tablespoon onto a greased baking sheet for a total of 12 cream puffs. Bake in a 400° oven about 30 minutes or till golden brown. Remove puffs to a wire rack; cool. Split puffs and remove any soft dough from inside.

**3** For filling.* place thawed cherries in a sieve over a 2-cup measuring cup; drain the cherries, reserving cherry juice. Add enough *water* to reserved cherry juice to make 2 cups liquid; set the cherries aside.

**4** In a large saucepan, stir together the sugar and cornstarch. Stir in cherry-juice mixture, kirsch or orange juice and red food coloring. Cook and stir over medium heat till thickened and bubbly. Cook and stir for 2 minutes more. Remove from heat; stir in vanilla and cherries. Cool to room temperature. (If you like, cover and refrigerate filling for up to 24 hours.)

**5** To assemble, spoon cherry filling inside puffs. Drizzle puffs with melted chocolate.** Serve with sweetened whipped cream. Makes 12 servings.

**\*Note:** To save time, substitute two *21-ounce cans cherry pie filling* for the cooked cherry filling.

**\*\*Note:** If you like, fill the puffs and drizzle with melted chocolate for up to 1 hour before serving. Cover and refrigerate till serving time.

## Make-Ahead Cream Puffs

If you're planning to serve cream puffs for a special occasion, make them ahead so there will be less work on party day. To store cream puffs overnight, seal the cooled shells in a plastic bag so they won't dry out. Keep them in the refrigerator for up to 24 hours. To freeze cream puffs, place the unfilled shells in an airtight container. Then, seal, label and freeze for 1 to 2 months. To thaw the shells, let them stand at room temperature for 5 to 10 minutes.

# STEAMED CRANBERRY PUDDING WITH HARD SAUCE

This moist, tangy steamed pudding traditionally highlights the Christmas brunch at Trillium Woods Bed and Breakfast in River Falls, Wisconsin. It's so extraordinary you'll want it to headline one of your yuletide menus, too.

1⅔ cups all-purpose flour
¾ teaspoon baking soda
½ teaspoon ground cinnamon
¼ teaspoon salt
¼ teaspoon ground nutmeg
⅔ cup sugar
½ cup shortening

2 beaten eggs
2 tablespoons light-flavored molasses
2½ cups coarsely chopped cranberries
Hard Sauce (recipe follows)

1 For pudding, in a medium mixing bowl, stir together flour, baking soda, cinnamon, salt and nutmeg. Set aside.

2 Well-grease and lightly flour a 1½-quart tall tower mold or casserole. Set aside. In a large mixing bowl, beat sugar and shortening with an electric mixer till light. Beat in eggs and molasses. Add flour mixture; beat till just combined. By hand, stir in cranberries. Turn into the prepared mold or casserole.

3 Cover mold or casserole with foil, pressing foil tightly against the rim of the mold. Place on a rack in a deep kettle. Add *boiling water* till water reaches 1 inch above the bottom of the mold. Cover kettle. Bring to a gentle boil. Steam for 3 to 3½ hours or till a wooden toothpick inserted near center comes out clean. If necessary, add more boiling water.

4 Cool on wire rack for 10 minutes. Unmold the pudding and cool for 30 minutes more. (Or, wrap and store in the refrigerator for up to 2 weeks. To reheat before serving, wrap pudding in foil and place on a baking sheet. Bake in a 350° oven for 30 to 40 minutes or till heated through.) Serve warm pudding with warm Hard Sauce. Makes 8 to 10 servings.

**Hard Sauce:** In a heavy medium saucepan, cook and stir 1 cup *sugar*, ½ cup *half-and-half* or *light cream* and ½ cup *butter* till the butter is melted and the mixture is smooth. Remove from heat; stir in ½ teaspoon *vanilla*. Serve warm with the pudding. Makes 1½ cups.

# SWEDISH PEAR TOSA

When the wind howls and the snow flies, the Jefferson-Day House in Hudson, Wisconsin, serves this fruit dish to warm its guests. The toasted almonds add crunch, while the raspberries add color.

6 Bartlett or other ripe, firm pears
1 tablespoon lemon juice
6 tablespoons butter
½ cup sugar
4½ teaspoons all-purpose flour

½ cup sliced almonds, toasted
¼ cup whipping cream, half-and-half or light cream
Frozen raspberries, thawed, or fresh red raspberries

1 Peel, core and slice the pears. Place them in a buttered 2-quart rectangular (11×7×1½-inch) baking dish. Sprinkle the pears with lemon juice.

2 In a small saucepan, melt the 6 tablespoons butter. Stir in sugar and flour. Cook and stir over medium heat for 4 to 5 minutes or till thick and smooth.

3 Remove from heat and stir in almonds and cream. Carefully pour the hot mixture over the pears.

4 Bake in a 375° oven about 25 minutes or till pears are tender. Serve warm. Top each serving with some raspberries. Makes 6 servings.

# GINGERBREAD PUDDING WITH BRANDY CREAM SAUCE

Nothing chases the winter chills away better than this heart-warming dessert from Quivey's Grove restaurant in Madison, Wisconsin. Don't forget the Brandy Cream Sauce—it's a must.

⅓ cup sugar
1 egg
⅓ cup butter, melted
2 cups all-purpose flour
1 teaspoon ground ginger
1 teaspoon ground
   cinnamon
¾ teaspoon baking soda

¼ teaspoon salt
¾ cup hot water
⅓ cup molasses
3 tablespoons honey
   Brandy Cream Sauce
     (recipe follows)
   Ground nutmeg (optional)

**1** In a large mixing bowl, beat sugar and egg with an electric mixer about 4 minutes or till fluffy. Add melted butter; beat well.

**2** In a medium bowl, stir together the flour, ginger, cinnamon, baking soda and salt. In a small bowl, combine hot water, molasses and honey. Add flour mixture and molasses mixture alternately to egg mixture, beating after each addition till just combined.

**3** Lightly grease eight 6-ounce custard cups; fill ⅔ full with batter. Cover each cup tightly with lightly greased foil. Place in a baking pan on an oven rack. Pour *boiling water* into the baking pan around the cups about halfway up the sides of the cups.

**4** Bake in a 350° oven about 45 minutes or till the puddings spring back when touched lightly with your finger. If necessary, add more boiling water to the pan. Cool on a wire rack for 5 minutes. Unmold the puddings; cool for 15 to 20 minutes more. Serve warm with Brandy Cream Sauce. If you like, sprinkle with nutmeg. Makes 8 servings.

**Brandy Cream Sauce:** In a mixing bowl, beat ¾ cup *whipping cream* and ¼ cup sifted *powdered sugar* till soft peaks form (tips curl). Stir in 1 tablespoon *brandy*. Cover and store in the refrigerator. Makes 1½ cups.

# CARAMEL APPLE-WALNUT SQUARES

This caramel-topped apple favorite from the Harvest Homecoming festival in New Albany, Indiana, is delicious plain, but tastes even better with heaping scoops of cinnamon or vanilla ice cream.

1¾ cups all-purpose flour
1 cup quick-cooking rolled
   oats
½ cup packed brown sugar
½ teaspoon baking soda
½ teaspoon salt
1 cup butter
20 caramels

1 14-ounce can sweetened
   condensed milk
1 21-ounce can apple pie
   filling
1 cup chopped walnuts
   Cinnamon or vanilla ice
     cream

**1** For crust, in a mixing bowl, combine the flour, oats, brown sugar, baking soda and salt. Using a pastry blender, cut in butter till crumbly. Set aside *1 cup* of the mixture.

**2** Press the remaining mixture into a 13×9×2-inch baking pan. Bake in a 375° oven for 10 minutes.

**3** For caramel filling, in a heavy saucepan, melt the caramels with the sweetened condensed milk over low heat, stirring till smooth.

**4** Spoon apple pie filling over the crust. Top with caramel filling. Sprinkle reserved crumb mixture over caramel layer. Top with walnuts.

**5** Bake about 20 minutes more or till golden brown. Cool in pan on wire rack. To serve, cut into squares. Serve with ice cream. Makes 15 to 20 servings.

# ALMOND-KISSED HOT-CROSS BUNS

akers at The French Loaf in Columbus, Ohio, pipe the tops of these rich buns with an almond-flavored cross pattern. Although traditionally served on Good Friday, hot-cross buns are a welcome treat anytime.

¾ cup golden raisins
¾ cup sugar
½ cup shortening
1½ teaspoons salt
½ teaspoon ground
   cinnamon
2 eggs
1 egg yolk
6 to 6½ cups bread flour
1¼ cups warm water
   (105° to 115°)

2 packages active dry yeast
½ cup finely chopped
   candied fruit
½ cup butter
2 tablespoons powdered
   sugar
1 egg
¼ cup water
1½ teaspoons vanilla
½ teaspoon almond extract
1 cup all-purpose flour

**1** Pour *boiling water* over raisins to cover. Let stand for 10 minutes; drain well. Meanwhile, in large mixing bowl, beat sugar, shortening, salt and cinnamon with electric mixer. Beat in the 2 eggs and egg yolk. Add 2¼ cups of the bread flour, the 1¼ cups warm water and the yeast. Beat with electric mixer on low speed for 30 seconds, scraping sides of bowl. Beat on high speed for 3 minutes. Using a wooden spoon, stir in the candied fruit, drained raisins and as much of the remaining bread flour as you can.

**2** Turn dough out onto a lightly floured surface. Knead in enough of the remaining bread flour to make a moderately stiff dough that is smooth and elastic (6 to 8 minutes total). Shape into a ball. Place in a greased bowl, turning once. Cover; let rise in a warm place till doubled (about 1½ hours).

**3** Grease two 13×9×2-inch baking pans. Punch dough down. Divide into 4 portions. Divide each portion into 10 pieces. Shape pieces into balls. Arrange balls in prepared pans, leaving a finger width between each. Cover; let rise till almost doubled (about 1 hour).

**4** Meanwhile, for cross batter, in a medium bowl, stir together butter and powdered sugar. Add the egg, the ¼ cup water, vanilla and almond extract. Add ¼ cup of the all-purpose flour; beat till smooth. Stir in the remaining all-purpose flour. If necessary, stir in more *water* to make a thick batter for piping. Spoon batter into pastry bag fitted with a ¼-inch round tip. Pipe a cross on each dough ball. Bake in 375° oven for 18 to 20 minutes or till golden brown. Makes 40 buns.

# MANDEL BREAD

akeries in Chicago, Illinois, prepare for Hanukkah with this cookielike bread. It will remind you of Italian biscotti, which is also baked once, sliced, then baked again. The second baking crisps the slices.

¾ cup sugar
¾ cup cooking oil
3 eggs
3 cups all-purpose flour
1 teaspoon baking powder

1 cup chopped nuts
1 cup raisins
2 teaspoons finely shredded
   lemon peel
1 teaspoon almond extract

**1** Generously grease a large baking sheet. Set aside. In a large mixing bowl, stir together sugar, oil and eggs, stirring till the sugar dissolves.

**2** In medium bowl, combine flour and baking powder. Stir into egg mixture along with nuts, raisins, lemon peel and almond extract (dough will be sticky).

**3** Form dough into two 12×3-inch logs on prepared baking sheet. Bake in a 350° oven for 30 minutes.

**4** Remove the logs from the oven and bias-cut into 1-inch-thick slices. Arrange slices on baking sheet.

**5** Return to oven and bake for 10 to 12 minutes more or till lightly browned. Remove to wire racks; cool. Makes 24 to 28 slices.

# CINNAMON SWIRL BREAD

**F**resh baked cinnamon bread is a trademark of Welliver's restaurant in Hagerstown, Indiana. Here's our version of their scrumptious bread, filled with cinnamon sugar and glazed with Powdered Sugar Icing.

6¾ to 7¼ cups all-purpose
    flour
2 packages active dry yeast
1¾ cups milk
⅓ cup butter
¼ cup sugar
1 teaspoon salt

3 eggs
2 tablespoons butter, melted
1 cup sugar
1 tablespoon ground
    cinnamon
Powdered Sugar Icing
    (recipe follows)

**1** In a large mixing bowl, stir together *3 cups* of the flour and the yeast. Set aside.

**2** In a saucepan, heat the milk, the ⅓ cup butter, the ¼ cup sugar and the salt just till warm (120° to 130°) and butter is almost melted, stirring constantly. Add to flour mixture. Add eggs. Beat with an electric mixer on low speed for 30 seconds, scraping sides of bowl. Beat on high speed for 3 minutes. Using a spoon, stir in as much of the remaining flour as you can.

**3** Turn out onto a lightly floured surface. Knead in enough of the remaining flour to make a moderately stiff dough that is smooth and elastic (6 to 8 minutes total). Shape into a ball. Place in a lightly greased bowl; turn once. Cover and let rise in a warm place till doubled (about 1¼ hours).

**4** Punch dough down. Turn out onto a lightly floured surface. Divide dough in half. Cover and let rest for 10 minutes.

**5** Lightly grease two 9×5×3-inch loaf pans. Roll each half of dough into an 18×8-inch rectangle. Brush the entire surface lightly with the 2 tablespoons melted butter. Combine the 1 cup sugar and the cinnamon; sprinkle *half* of the mixture over each rectangle.

**6** Roll up each dough rectangle, jelly-roll style, starting from a short side. Seal. Place, sealed edges down, in the prepared pans. Cover and let rise in a warm place till nearly doubled (35 to 45 minutes).

**7** Bake in a 375° oven about 35 minutes or till bread sounds hollow when tapped. If necessary to prevent overbrowning, cover loosely with foil for the last 15 minutes of baking. Remove to wire racks; cool.

**8** Drizzle Powdered Sugar Icing over the warm bread. Makes 2 loaves.

**Powdered Sugar Icing:** Combine 2 cups sifted *powdered sugar*, 1 teaspoon *vanilla* and enough *milk* (about ¼ cup) to make of drizzling consistency.

# NORWEGIAN-STYLE SOUR CREAM TWISTS

**A** specialty of my late mother, Edythe Storvick, these twists are a tasty reminder of my Norwegian heritage," comments Arlene Wee of Huxley, Iowa. They are delicious both warm or cooled to room temperature.

3½ cups all-purpose flour
1 teaspoon salt
1 cup shortening
1 package active dry yeast
¼ cup warm water
    (105° to 115°)

¾ cup dairy sour cream
1 egg
2 egg yolks
1 teaspoon vanilla
    Sugar

**1** In a large bowl, combine flour and salt. Cut in shortening till pieces are size of small peas.

**2** Stir yeast into warm water to soften. Combine yeast mixture with sour cream, egg, egg yolks and vanilla. Add all at once to flour mixture. Mix well. Cover; refrigerate for 2 to 3 hours.

**3** Divide dough in half. On a well-sugared surface, roll *half* of dough into a 16×8-inch rectangle. Sprinkle with sugar. Fold in edges toward center. Repeat rolling, sprinkling and folding two more times, sprinkling work surface with sugar as needed. Roll again to form a 16×8-inch rectangle. Cut lengthwise into two 16×4-inch strips. Cut into thirty-two 4×1-inch strips. Twist each strip; place on ungreased baking sheet, pressing ends down slightly. Repeat with remaining dough. Bake in a 375° oven for 12 to 15 minutes or till done. Makes 64.

# IN A PINCH

There's no doubt that you'll get the best baking results when you use the specified ingredients. There's also no doubt that sooner or later you'll be caught short of something.

If you can't borrow that cup of sugar or few squares of unsweetened chocolate from your neighbor, here are some handy substitutions. You may notice a change in flavor or texture, so use these substitutions only in a pinch.

| Ingredient | Substitution |
| --- | --- |
| 1 cup cake flour | 1 cup minus 2 tablespoons all-purpose flour |
| 1 cup self-rising flour | 1 cup all-purpose flour plus 1 teaspoon baking powder, $\frac{1}{2}$ teaspoon salt and $\frac{1}{4}$ teaspoon baking soda |
| 1 cup sugar | 1 cup packed brown sugar |
| 1 teaspoon baking powder | $\frac{1}{2}$ teaspoon cream of tartar plus $\frac{1}{4}$ teaspoon baking soda |
| 1 cup buttermilk | 1 tablespoon lemon juice or vinegar plus enough milk to make 1 cup (let stand 5 minutes before using); 1 cup plain yogurt; or 1 cup milk plus $1\frac{3}{4}$ teaspoons cream of tartar |
| 1 cup half-and-half or light cream | 1 tablespoon melted butter plus enough milk to make 1 cup |
| 1 cup milk | $\frac{1}{2}$ cup evaporated milk plus $\frac{1}{2}$ cup water or 1 cup water plus $\frac{1}{3}$ cup nonfat dry milk powder |
| 1 cup corn syrup | 1 cup sugar plus $\frac{1}{4}$ cup water |
| 1 cup honey | $1\frac{1}{4}$ cups sugar plus $\frac{1}{4}$ cup water |
| 1 teaspoon apple pie spice | $\frac{1}{2}$ teaspoon ground cinnamon plus $\frac{1}{4}$ teaspoon ground nutmeg, $\frac{1}{8}$ teaspoon ground allspice and dash ground ginger |
| 1 teaspoon pumpkin pie spice | $\frac{1}{2}$ teaspoon ground cinnamon plus $\frac{1}{4}$ teaspoon ground ginger, $\frac{1}{4}$ teaspoon ground allspice and $\frac{1}{8}$ teaspoon ground nutmeg |
| 1 ounce semisweet chocolate | $\frac{1}{2}$ ounce unsweetened chocolate plus 1 tablespoon sugar or 3 tablespoons semisweet chocolate pieces |
| 4 ounces sweet baking chocolate | $\frac{1}{4}$ cup unsweetened cocoa powder plus $\frac{1}{3}$ cup sugar and 3 tablespoons shortening |
| 1 ounce unsweetened chocolate | 3 tablespoons unsweetened cocoa powder plus 1 tablespoon shortening or cooking oil |

# NEVER-FAIL CINNAMON ROLLS

his is a traditional Christmas Eve treat at the home of former North Dakota Governor George Sinner. They are worth every moment spent making them. For best results, always double-check that the yeast you use is fresh.

5¼ to 5¾ cups all-purpose
    flour
1 package active dry yeast
1½ cups water or milk
¼ cup sugar
¼ cup shortening
1 teaspoon salt

2 eggs
½ cup sugar
2 teaspoons ground
    cinnamon
2 tablespoons butter,
    melted
Icing (recipe follows)

**1** In a large mixing bowl, combine *2½ cups* of the flour and the yeast. In a saucepan, heat the water or milk, the ¼ cup sugar, shortening and salt just till warm (120° to 130°) and shortening is almost melted, stirring constantly. Add to flour mixture. Add eggs. Beat with an electric mixer on low speed for 30 seconds, scraping sides of bowl. Beat on high speed for 3 minutes. Using a wooden spoon, stir in as much of the remaining flour as you can.

**2** Turn dough out onto a lightly floured surface. Knead in enough of the remaining flour to make a moderately soft dough that is smooth and elastic (3 to 5 minutes total). Shape into a ball. Place in a lightly greased bowl; turn once. Cover and let rise in a warm place till doubled (45 minutes to 1 hour).

**3** Punch dough down. Turn out onto a lightly floured surface. Divide in half. Cover and let rest for 10 minutes. Grease three 9×1½-inch round baking pans. (Or, grease three 8×8×2-inch baking pans.) Set aside. In a small bowl, combine the ½ cup sugar and the cinnamon. Set cinnamon-sugar mixture aside. Roll each half of the dough into a 12×8-inch rectangle. Brush rectangles with the melted butter. Sprinkle with cinnamon-sugar mixture. Roll up each, jelly-roll style, beginning from a long side. Seal. Slice each roll of dough into 12 pieces. Arrange eight dough pieces, cut sides up, in each of the prepared pans. Cover; let rise in a warm place till nearly doubled (about 30 minutes).

**4** Bake in 375° oven for 20 to 25 minutes or till golden brown. Cool slightly on wire racks. Remove from pans. Drizzle with Icing. Serve warm. Makes 24 rolls.

**Icing:** Combine 1 cup sifted *powdered sugar*, a few drops *almond extract* and enough *milk* (2 to 3 teaspoons) to make icing of drizzling consistency.

# BAY VIEW INN'S HERB ROLLS

uests munch these cheese-filled rolls at the Bay View Inn in Petoskey, Michigan, as they gaze out onto Little Traverse Bay. If you like, try another fresh herb option, such as basil or thyme, instead of the parsley for variety.

3 to 3½ cups bread flour
1 package active dry yeast
1 cup milk
¼ cup sugar
¼ cup butter
1 clove garlic, minced
½ teaspoon salt
1 egg

1 cup shredded provolone
    cheese (4 ounces)
¾ cup grated Parmesan
    cheese (3 ounces)
1 tablespoon snipped fresh
    parsley
2 teaspoons snipped fresh
    chives

**1** In a large bowl, combine *1½ cups* of the flour and the yeast. In a saucepan, combine milk, sugar, butter, garlic and salt. Heat and stir just till warm (120° to 130°) and butter almost melts; add to flour mixture. Add egg. Beat with electric mixer on low speed for 30 seconds, scraping bowl. Beat on high speed 3 minutes. Stir in cheeses, parsley and chives. Using spoon, stir in as much remaining flour as you can.

**2** Turn dough onto lightly floured surface. Knead in enough of the remaining flour to make moderately stiff dough that is smooth and elastic (6 to 8 minutes total). Shape into ball. Place in greased bowl; turn once. Cover; let rise till doubled (about 1 hour).

**3** Lightly grease baking sheets. Set aside. Punch dough down. Turn out onto lightly floured surface. Divide dough in half. Cover; let rest for 10 minutes. Divide each half into 12 pieces; shape into rolls. Place on prepared sheets. Cover; let rise in warm place till nearly doubled (about 30 minutes). Bake in 325° oven about 20 minutes or till golden brown. Makes 24 rolls.

# APPLESAUCE-DATE COFFEE CAKE

This Midwestern favorite is better for you than other classic coffee cakes. Less fat, added wheat bran and naturally sweet dates help make it so. Serve it for brunch with a fruit cup and your favorite flavored coffee or tea.

Nonstick spray coating
1⅓ cups all-purpose flour
⅔ cup packed brown sugar
½ cup snipped pitted whole dates or mixed dried fruit bits
¼ cup unprocessed wheat bran
2 teaspoons baking powder
1 teaspoon grated orange peel

¼ teaspoon salt
¾ cup unsweetened applesauce
¼ cup skim milk
¼ cup refrigerated or frozen egg product, thawed, or 1 beaten egg
2 tablespoons cooking oil
⅓ cup broken pecans
Apple Icing (recipe follows)

1 Spray a 9×9×2-inch baking pan with nonstick coating. Set aside.

2 In a large mixing bowl, stir together the flour, brown sugar, snipped dates or mixed dried fruit bits, wheat bran, baking powder, orange peel and salt. Make a well in the center. Set aside.

3 In a medium mixing bowl, stir together applesauce, milk, egg product or egg and oil. Add all at once to flour mixture, stirring till just combined.

4 Spread into the bottom of the prepared pan. Sprinkle the pecans over.

5 Bake in a 375° oven for 20 to 30 minutes or till a wooden toothpick inserted in center comes out clean. Cool slightly on a wire rack. Drizzle with Apple Icing. Serve warm. Makes 9 servings.

**Apple Icing:** Stir together ½ cup sifted *powdered sugar* and enough *apple* or *orange juice* (1 to 2 teaspoons) to make of drizzling consistency.

# Can't-Miss Coffee Cakes

Sharing the latest news over a piece of coffee cake and a steaming cup of coffee is a Heartland custom that dates back several decades. For delicate, tender coffee cakes that would make even the fussiest old-time cook proud, remember these coffee cake making dos and don'ts:

♦ When your recipe calls for a baking pan, be sure to use a shiny one. The shiny surface reflects the heat producing a coffee cake with a golden, tender crust.

♦ Most coffee cakes are delicious served warm, but not hot right out of the oven. To achieve the perfect eating temperature, let the coffee cake cool for 20 to 30 minutes before serving.

♦ To store leftover coffee cake, place the cake in a tightly covered container and store it at room temperature. If the coffee cake contains cream cheese, cover and store it in the refrigerator.

# LEMONY TEA BREAD

erbs subtly flavor this bread that Lynne Harshbarger slices for afternoon tea at The Flower Patch bed-and-breakfast in Arcola, Illinois. She prefers lemon balm and lemon thyme, but you can use lemon peel and regular thyme.

¾ cup milk
1 tablespoon finely snipped
   fresh lemon balm
   or 1 teaspoon finely
   shredded lemon peel
1 tablespoon finely snipped
   fresh lemon thyme or
   regular thyme or
   1 teaspoon dried
   thyme, crushed
2 cups all-purpose flour

1½ teaspoons baking powder
¼ teaspoon salt
1 cup sugar
⅓ cup butter
2 eggs
2 tablespoons finely
   shredded lemon peel
⅔ cup sifted powdered
   sugar
1 tablespoon lemon juice

**1** Grease and flour a 9×5×3-inch loaf pan. Set aside. In a small saucepan, heat milk, lemon balm or lemon peel, and lemon thyme or thyme till just warm. Remove from heat; cool. Meanwhile, stir together the flour, baking powder and salt. Set aside.

**2** In a large mixing bowl, beat sugar and butter till thoroughly combined. Add eggs, one at a time, beating till fluffy. Add the milk mixture and the flour mixture alternately to egg mixture, beating on low speed till just combined. Fold in the 2 tablespoons lemon peel.

**3** Turn into the prepared pan. Bake in a 350° oven for 45 to 50 minutes or till wooden toothpick inserted in center comes out clean. Cool on wire rack for 10 minutes. Remove from the pan; cool completely on wire rack.

**4** Combine powdered sugar and enough of the lemon juice to make of drizzling consistency. Drizzle over bread. Makes 1 loaf.

# MAPLE-PECAN SCONES

he Inn at Cedar Crossing in Door County, Wisconsin, features these scones made with Wisconsin pure maple syrup. They're scrumptious slathered with butter and served with a cold glass of milk.

3 cups all-purpose flour
1 cup chopped pecans
4 teaspoons baking powder
¼ teaspoon salt
¾ cup butter

½ cup pure maple syrup or
   maple-flavored syrup
½ cup milk
Pure maple syrup or
   maple-flavored syrup

**1** In a large mixing bowl, stir together the flour, pecans, baking powder and salt. Using a pastry blender, cut in butter till mixture resembles cornmeal.

**2** In a small mixing bowl, combine the ½ cup maple syrup and the milk. Add to the flour mixture; stir till just combined.

**3** On floured surface, roll dough to ¾-inch thickness. Cut with a 2½-inch biscuit cutter. Place on ungreased baking sheet. Brush with additional maple syrup. Bake in a 375° oven about 15 minutes or till golden brown. Makes 12 scones.

# HONEY-RHUBARB MUFFINS

ernie Brand, a vendor from Shoreview, Minnesota, sells honey at St. Paul's historic Lowertown neighborhood farmers' market. He recommends serving Whipped Honey Butter on these fruit-filled muffins.

| | |
|---|---|
| 1 tablespoon butter | 1 teaspoon baking soda |
| ½ cup sugar | ½ teaspoon salt |
| 1 slightly beaten egg | ¾ cup sour milk* |
| 1 cup packed brown sugar | 1½ cups chopped rhubarb |
| ⅔ cup cooking oil | (use fresh or frozen) |
| ½ cup honey | ½ cup chopped nuts |
| ½ teaspoon vanilla | Whipped Honey Butter |
| 2½ cups all-purpose flour | (recipe follows) |

**1** For topping, using a pastry blender, cut butter into sugar till mixture resembles coarse crumbs. Set mixture aside.

**2** For muffins, line twenty-one 2½-inch muffin cups with paper bake cups. Set aside. In a large bowl, combine egg, brown sugar, oil, honey and vanilla.

**3** In a medium mixing bowl, stir together the flour, baking soda and salt. Add flour mixture and sour milk alternately to the egg mixture, stirring after each addition till moistened (batter should be lumpy). Gently fold in the rhubarb and nuts.

**4** Fill prepared muffin cups ⅔ full with batter. Sprinkle with the topping. Bake in a 325° oven for 35 to 40 minutes or till golden brown. Remove from pans. Serve warm or cool with Whipped Honey Butter. Makes about 21 muffins.

**Whipped Honey Butter:** In small mixing bowl, combine ½ cup softened *butter* and ¼ teaspoon finely shredded *lemon peel*. Gradually add ¼ cup *honey*, beating with an electric mixer on high speed till fluffy. Cover and store in the refrigerator. Let butter mixture stand at room temperature about 1 hour before serving.

**\*Note:** To make sour milk, place 2 teaspoons *lemon juice* in a glass measuring cup. Pour in enough *milk* to make ¾ cup liquid. Stir and let stand for 5 minutes.

---

# BREAKFAST PUFFS

any Amish cooks in the Heartland make puffs similar to these. Roll them in melted butter and a cinnamon-sugar mixture, then listen to the good-morning chorus of "Mmmmmm!"

| | |
|---|---|
| 1½ cups all-purpose flour | 1 teaspoon vanilla |
| 1½ teaspoons baking powder | ½ cup milk |
| ½ teaspoon salt | ½ cup sugar |
| ¼ teaspoon ground mace or | 1 teaspoon ground |
| nutmeg | cinnamon |
| 1 beaten egg | 6 tablespoons butter, |
| ½ cup sugar | melted |
| ⅓ cup cooking oil | |

**1** Grease ten 2½-inch muffin cups. Set aside. In a large mixing bowl, stir together the flour, baking powder, salt and mace or nutmeg.

**2** In a small mixing bowl, beat egg, ½ cup sugar, the oil and vanilla with an electric mixer on medium speed for 30 seconds. Add the flour mixture and milk alternately to egg mixture, beating on low speed after each addition till just combined. Fill prepared muffin cups ⅔ full with batter.

**3** Bake in a 350° oven for 15 to 20 minutes or till tops of muffins are firm and golden brown.

**4** Meanwhile, in a shallow bowl, combine ½ cup sugar and the cinnamon. Remove muffins from pans while still hot; roll in melted butter, then in cinnamon-sugar mixture. Serve immediately. Makes 10 puffs.

HONEY-RHUBARB
MUFFINS

# INDEX

*Numbers in bold type indicate a photograph.*

## METRIC COOKING HINTS

By making a few conversions, cooks in Australia, Canada, and the United Kingdom can use the recipes in *Heartland Baking* with confidence. The charts on this page provide a guide for converting measurements from the U.S. customary system, which is used throughout this book, to the imperial and metric systems. There also is a conversion table for oven temperatures to accommodate the differences in oven calibrations.

**Product Differences:** Most of the ingredients called for in the recipes in this book are available in English-speaking countries. However, some are known by different names. Here are some common American ingredients and their possible counterparts:
■ Sugar is granulated or castor sugar.
■ Powdered sugar is icing sugar.
■ All-purpose flour is plain household flour or white flour. When self-rising flour is used in place of all-purpose flour in a recipe that calls for leavening, omit the leavening agent (baking soda or baking powder) and salt.
■ Light corn syrup is golden syrup.
■ Cornstarch is cornflour.
■ Baking soda is bicarbonate of soda.
■ Vanilla is vanilla essence.
■ Green, red, or yellow sweet peppers are capsicums.
■ Golden raisins are sultanas.

**Volume and Weight:** Americans traditionally use cup measures for liquid and solid ingredients. The chart, *top right*, shows the approximate imperial and metric equivalents. If you are accustomed to weighing solid ingredients, the following approximate equivalents will be helpful.
■ 1 cup butter, castor sugar, or rice = 8 ounces = about 250 grams
■ 1 cup flour = 4 ounces = about 125 grams
■ 1 cup icing sugar = 5 ounces = about 150 grams
  Spoon measures are used for smaller amounts of ingredients. Although the size of the tablespoon varies slightly in different countries, for practical purposes and for recipes in this book, a straight substitution is all that's necessary.
  Measurements made using cups or spoons always should be level unless stated otherwise.

## EQUIVALENTS: U.S. = AUST[E]

⅛ teaspoon = 0.5 ml
¼ teaspoon = 1 ml
½ teaspoon = 2 ml
1 teaspoon = 5 ml
1 tablespoon = 15 ml
¼ cup = 2 fluid ounces = 60 ml
⅓ cup = 3 fluid ounces = 90 ml
½ cup = 4 fluid ounces = 120 ml
⅔ cup = 5 fluid ounces = 150 ml
¾ cup = 6 fluid ounces = 180 ml
1 cup = 8 fluid ounces = 240 ml
2 cups = 16 fluid ounces (1 pint) = 475 ml
1 quart = 32 fluid ounces (2 pints) = 1 litre
½ inch = 1.27 cm
1 inch = 2.54 cm

## BAKING PAN SIZES

| American | Metric |
|---|---|
| 8×1½-inch round baking pan | 20×4-cm cake |
| 9×1½-inch round baking pan | 23×3.5-cm ca |
| 11×7×1½-inch baking pan | 28×18×4-cm |
| 13×9×2-inch baking pan | 30×20×3-cm |
| 2-quart rectangular baking dish | 30×20×3-cm |
| 15×10×2-inch baking pan | 30×25×2-cm (Swiss roll |
| 9-inch pie plate | 22×4- or 23×4 |
| 7- or 8-inch springform pan | 18- or 20-cm s loose-botto |
| 9×5×3-inch loaf pan | 23×13×7-cm o narrow loa or paté tin |
| 1½-quart casserole | 1.5-litre casser |
| 2-quart casserole | 2-litre cassero |

## OVEN TEMPERATURE EQUIVA[LENTS]

| Fahrenheit Setting | Celsius Setting* | Gas Setting |
|---|---|---|
| 300°F | 150°C | Gas Mark 2 (slo |
| 325°F | 160°C | Gas Mark 3 (mo |
| 350°F | 180°C | Gas Mark 4 (mo |
| 375°F | 190°C | Gas Mark 5 (mo |
| 400°F | 200°C | Gas Mark 6 (hot |
| 425°F | 220°C | Gas Mark 7 |
| 450°F | 230°C | Gas Mark 8 (ver |
| Broil | | Grill |

* Electric and gas ovens may be calibrated using
However, for an electric oven, increase the Celsiu
20° when cooking above 160°C. For convection o
ovens (gas or electric), lower the temperature set
cooking at all heat levels.

## METRIC COOKING HINTS

By making a few conversions, cooks in Australia, Canada, and the United Kingdom can use the recipes in *Heartland Baking* with confidence. The charts on this page provide a guide for converting measurements from the U.S. customary system, which is used throughout this book, to the imperial and metric systems. There also is a conversion table for oven temperatures to accommodate the differences in oven calibrations.

**Product Differences:** Most of the ingredients called for in the recipes in this book are available in English-speaking countries. However, some are known by different names. Here are some common American ingredients and their possible counterparts:
- Sugar is granulated or castor sugar.
- Powdered sugar is icing sugar.
- All-purpose flour is plain household flour or white flour. When self-rising flour is used in place of all-purpose flour in a recipe that calls for leavening, omit the leavening agent (baking soda or baking powder) and salt.
- Light corn syrup is golden syrup.
- Cornstarch is cornflour.
- Baking soda is bicarbonate of soda.
- Vanilla is vanilla essence.
- Green, red, or yellow sweet peppers are capsicums.
- Golden raisins are sultanas.

**Volume and Weight:** Americans traditionally use cup measures for liquid and solid ingredients. The chart, *top right*, shows the approximate imperial and metric equivalents. If you are accustomed to weighing solid ingredients, the following approximate equivalents will be helpful.
- 1 cup butter, castor sugar, or rice = 8 ounces = about 250 grams
- 1 cup flour = 4 ounces = about 125 grams
- 1 cup icing sugar = 5 ounces = about 150 grams

Spoon measures are used for smaller amounts of ingredients. Although the size of the tablespoon varies slightly in different countries, for practical purposes and for recipes in this book, a straight substitution is all that's necessary.

Measurements made using cups or spoons always should be level unless stated otherwise.

## EQUIVALENTS: U.S. = AUSTRALIA/U.K.

⅛ teaspoon = 0.5 ml
¼ teaspoon = 1 ml
½ teaspoon = 2 ml
1 teaspoon = 5 ml
1 tablespoon = 15 ml
¼ cup = 2 fluid ounces = 60 ml
⅓ cup = 3 fluid ounces = 90 ml
½ cup = 4 fluid ounces = 120 ml
⅔ cup = 5 fluid ounces = 150 ml
¾ cup = 6 fluid ounces = 180 ml
1 cup = 8 fluid ounces = 240 ml
2 cups = 16 fluid ounces (1 pint) = 475 ml
1 quart = 32 fluid ounces (2 pints) = 1 litre
½ inch = 1.27 cm
1 inch = 2.54 cm

## BAKING PAN SIZES

| American | Metric |
| --- | --- |
| 8×1½-inch round baking pan | 20×4-cm cake tin |
| 9×1½-inch round baking pan | 23×3.5-cm cake tin |
| 11×7×1½-inch baking pan | 28×18×4-cm baking tin |
| 13×9×2-inch baking pan | 30×20×3-cm baking tin |
| 2-quart rectangular baking dish | 30×20×3-cm baking tin |
| 15×10×2-inch baking pan | 30×25×2-cm baking tin (Swiss roll tin) |
| 9-inch pie plate | 22×4- or 23×4-cm pie plate |
| 7- or 8-inch springform pan | 18- or 20-cm springform or loose-bottom cake tin |
| 9×5×3-inch loaf pan | 23×13×7-cm or 2-pound narrow loaf tin or paté tin |
| 1½-quart casserole | 1.5-litre casserole |
| 2-quart casserole | 2-litre casserole |

## OVEN TEMPERATURE EQUIVALENTS

| Fahrenheit Setting | Celsius Setting* | Gas Setting |
| --- | --- | --- |
| 300°F | 150°C | Gas Mark 2 (slow) |
| 325°F | 160°C | Gas Mark 3 (moderately slow) |
| 350°F | 180°C | Gas Mark 4 (moderate) |
| 375°F | 190°C | Gas Mark 5 (moderately hot) |
| 400°F | 200°C | Gas Mark 6 (hot) |
| 425°F | 220°C | Gas Mark 7 |
| 450°F | 230°C | Gas Mark 8 (very hot) |
| Broil | | Grill |

* Electric and gas ovens may be calibrated using Celsius. However, for an electric oven, increase the Celsius setting 10° to 20° when cooking above 160°C. For convection or forced-air ovens (gas or electric), lower the temperature setting 10°C when cooking at all heat levels.